John Aikin

A View of the Character and Public Services of the Late John Howard

John Aikin

A View of the Character and Public Services of the Late John Howard

ISBN/EAN: 9783337400200

Printed in Europe, USA, Canada, Australia, Japan

Cover: Foto ©Suzi / pixelio.de

More available books at **www.hansebooks.com**

A VIEW

OF THE

CHARACTER AND PUBLIC SERVICES

OF THE LATE

JOHN HOWARD, Esq.

LL. D. F. R. S.

By JOHN AIKIN, M.D.

In commune auxilium natus, ac publicum bonum, ex quo dabit
cuique partem : etiam ad calamitofos, pro portione, improbandos
et emendandos, bonitatem fuam permittet.   SENECA.

LONDON:

PRINTED FOR J. JOHNSON, NO. 72, ST. PAUL'S CHURCH-YARD.

MDCCXCII.

V I E W

OF THE

C H A R A C T E R, &c.

***

I F it be a juft obfervation, that every man who has attained uncommon emi-nence in his particular line of purfuit, becomes an object worthy of the pub lic notice, how forcibly muft fuch a maxim apply to that fpecies of excel-lence which renders a man the greateft benefactor to his fellow-creatures, and the nobleft fubject of their contempla-tion? Beneficence, pure in its inten-tions, wife and comprehenfive in its plans, and active and fuccefsful in exe-

B   cution,

cution, muſt ever ſtand at the head of thoſe qualities which elevate the human character; and mankind cannot have a concern ſo important, as the. diffuſion of ſuch a ſpirit, by means of the moſt perfect and impreſſive examples, in which it has actually been diſplayed.

Among thoſe truly illuſtrious perſons who, in the ſeveral ages and nations of the world, have marked their track through life by a continued courſe of *doing good*, few have been ſo diſtinguiſhed, either by the extent of the good produced, or the purity of motive and energy of character exhibited in the proceſs of doing it, as the late Mr. HOWARD... To have adopted the cauſe of the priſoner, the ſick, and the deſtitute, not only in his own country,

but

but throughout all Europe;—to have confiderably alleviated the burden of prefent mifery among thofe unfortunate claffes, and at the fame time to have provided for the reformation of the vicious, and the prevention of future crimes and calamities;—to have been inftrumental in the actual eftablifhment of many plans of humanity and utility, and to have laid the foundation for much more improvement hereafter; —and to have done all this as a private unaided individual, ftruggling with toils, dangers, and difficulties, which might have appalled the moft refolute; is furely a range of beneficence which fcarcely ever before came within the compafs of one man's exertions. Juftly, then, does the name of *Howard* ftand among

thofe

thofe which confer 'the higheft honour on the Englifh character; and, fince his actions cannot fail to tranfmit his memory with glory to pofterity, it is incumbent on his countrymen and cotemporaries, for their own fakes, to tranfmit correfponding memorials of their veneration and gratitude.

It would, indeed, be a convincing proof of the increafed good fenfe and virtue of the age, if fuch characters as this were found to rife in the comparative fcale of fame and applaufe. Long enough has mankind weakly paid its admiration as the reward of pernicious exertions,— of talents, often very moderate in themfelves, and only rendered confpicuous by the blaze of mifchief they have kindled. It is now furely

time

time that men should know and diftinguifh their benefactors from their foes;
and that the nobleft incitements to action
fhould be given to thofe actions only
which are directed to the general welfare.

Since the lamented death of this excellent perfon, there have not been wanting refpectable eulogies of his character,
and fuch biographical notices concerning
him, as might in fome meafure gratify
that public curiofity which is awakened
by every celebrated name. There is yet
wanting, however, what I confider as by
much the moft valuable tribute to the
memory of every man diftinguifhed by
public fervices; I mean, a portraiture
of him, modelled upon thofe circumftances which rendered him eminent;

difplaying

difplaying in their rife and progrefs thofe
features of character which fo peculiarly
fitted him for the part he undertook, the
origin and gradual developement of his
great defigns, and all the fucceffive fteps
by which they were brought to their
final ftate of maturity. It is this branch
of biographical writing that alone entitles
it to rank high among the compofi-
tions relative to human life and manners. Nature, indeed, has implanted
in us a defire of becoming acquainted
with thofe circumftances belonging to a
diftinguifhed character which are common to him and the herd of mankind;
and it is therefore right that fuch a defire fhould in fome degree be gratified;
but to make *that* the principal object of
attention, which, but for its affociation

3   with

with fomewhat more important, would not at all deferve notice, is furely to reverfe the value of things, and to eftimate the mafs by the quantity of its alloy, rather than by that of the precious metal.

The deficiency which I have ftated relative to Mr. *Howard*, it is my prefent object, as far as I am able, to fupply; and however the tafk in fome refpect may be beyond my powers, yet the advantage I enjoyed of a long and confidential intercourfe with him during the publication of his works, and of frequent converfation with him concerning the paft and future objects of his enquiries, together with the communications with which I have been favoured by fome of his moft intimate friends,—will, I hope,

B 4   juftify

juftify me in the eye of the public for taking it upon myfelf. I truft I have already appeared not infenfible to his exalted merit, nor indifferent to his reputation.

One thing more I think it neceffary to fay concerning this attempt. It has been more than once fuggefted in print, but, I believe, without any foundation, that a life of Mr. *Howard* might be expected to appear under the fanction and authority of his *family*. It is proper for me to avow, that this is not *that* work. The undertaking is perfectly fpontaneous on my part, without encouragement from his relations or reprefentatives. Mr. *Howard* was a man with whom every one capable of feeling the excellence and dignity of his character,

4 might

might claim kindred; and *they* were the neareft to him whom he made the confidents and depofitaries of his defigns.

JOHN HOWARD was born, according to the beft information I am able to obtain, about the year 1727. His father was an upholfterer and carpet-warehoufeman in Long-lane, Smithfield, who; having acquired a handfome fortune, retired from bufinefs, and had a houfe firft at Enfield and afterwards at Hackney. It was, I believe, at the former of thefe places that Mr. *Howard* was born.

As Mr. *Howard*'s father was a ftrict proteftant diffenter, it was natural for him to educate his fon under a preceptor of the fame principles. But his choice for this purpofe was the fource of a lafting misfortune, which, as it has been

too

too frequent an occurrence, deserves particular notice. There was at that time a
schoolmaster at some distance from London, who, in consequence of his moral
and religious character, had been in-
trusted with the education of the children of most of the opulent dissenters in
the metropolis, though extremely deficient in the qualifications requisite for
such an office *. That persons whose
own education and habits of life have
rendered them very inadequate judges of

* I find it asserted in some memoirs of Mr.
Howard in the *Universal Magazine*, that this person
(whose name is there mentioned) was a man of
considerable learning, and author of a translation
of the New Testament and of a Latin grammar.
Without inquiring how far this may set aside the
charge of his being deficient as an instructor, I
think it proper to say, that my only foundation
for that charge is Mr. *Howard*'s own authority.

the

the talents neceffary for an inftructor of
youth, fhould eafily fall into this error,
is not to be wondered at; but the evil is
a real one, though its caufe be excufe-
able: and, as fmall communities with
ftrong party attachments are peculiarly
liable to this mifplaced confidence, it is
right that they fhould in a particular
manner be put on their guard againft
it. They who know the diffenters will
acknowledge, that none appear more
fenfible of the importance of a good
education, or lefs fparing in their endeavours to procure it for their children;
nor, upon the whole, can it be faid that
they are unfuccefsful in their attempts.
Indeed, the very confined fyftem of inftruction adopted in the public fchools
of this kingdom, renders it no difficult
                                                    talk

tafk to vie with them in the attainment
of objects of real utility. But if it
be made a leading purpofe to train
up youth in a certain fet of opinions,
and for this end it be thought effential
that the mafter fhould be exclufively
chofen from among thofe who are the
moft clofely attached to them; it is obvious that a fmall community muft lie
under great comparative difadvantages.

The event with refpect to Mr. *Howard*
was (as he has affured me, with greater
indignation than I have heard him exprefs upon many fubjects), that, after a
continuance of feven years at this fchool,
he left it not fully taught any one thing.
The lofs of this period was irreparable;
he felt it all his life after, and it was but
too obvious to thofe who converfed with
him,

him. From this school he was removed
to Mr. Eames's academy; but his continuance there muft, I conceive, have
been of fhort duration; and, whatever
might be his acquifitions in that place,
he certainly did not fupply the deficiencies of his earlier education. As
fome of the accounts publifhed concerning him, might inculcate the idea that
he had attained confiderable proficiency
in letters, I feel myfelf obliged, from
my own knowledge, to affert, that he
was never able to fpeak or write his
native language with grammatical cor-
rectnefs, and that his acquaintance with
other languages (the French, perhaps,
excepted) was flight and fuperficial.
In eftimating the powers of his mind,
it rather adds to the account, that he

had

had this additional difficulty to combat in his purfuit of the great objects of his later years.

Mr. *Howard*'s father died when he was young, and bequeathed to him and a daughter, his only children, confiderable fortunes. He directed in his will, that his fon fhould not come to the poffef-fion of his property till his twenty-fifth year.

It was, probably, in confequence of the father's direction that he was bound apprentice to a wholefale grocer in the city. This will appear a fingular ftep in the education of a young man of for-tune; but, at that period, inuring youth to habits of method and induftry, and giving them a prudent regard to money, with a knowledge of the modes of em-

ploying

ploying it to advantage, were by many confidered as the moſt important points in every condition of life. Mr. *Howard* was probably indebted to this part, of his education for ſome of that ſpirit of order, and knowledge of common affairs, which he poſſeſſed; but he did not in this ſituation contract any of that love of aggrandiſement which is the baſis of all commercial exertions; and ſo irkſome was the employment to him, that, on coming of age, he bought out the remainder of his time, and immediately ſet out on his travels to France and Italy.

On his return he mixed with the world, and lived in the ſtyle of other young men of leiſure and fortune. He had acquired that taſte for the arts which the

the view of the moft perfect examples of them is fitted to create; and, notwithftand-ing the defects of his education, he was not without an attachment to reading and the ftudy of nature. The delicacy of his conftitution, however, induced him to take lodgings in the country, where for fome time his health was the prin-cipal object of his attention. As he was fuppofed to be of a confumptive habit, he was put upon a rigorous regimen of diet, which laid the foundation of that extraordinary abftemioufnefs and indiffer-ence to the gratifications of the palate which ever after fo much diftinguifhed him. It is probable that, from his firft appearance in a ftate of independence, his way of thinking and acting was marked by a certain fingularity. Of this, one

of

of the moft remarkable confequences
was his firft marriage about his twenty-
fifth year. As a return of gratitude to
Mrs. *Sarah Lardeau* (or *Loidore*), widow,
with whom he lodged at Stoke Newington, for her kind attention to him during his invalid ftate, he propofed marriage to her, though fhe was twice his
age, and extremely fickly; and, notwithftanding her remonftrances on the
impropriety of fuch an union, he per-
fifted in his defign, and it took place.
She is reprefented as a fenfible, worthy
woman; and on her death, three years
afterwards (during which interval he continued at Newington), Mr. *Howard* was
fincerely affected with his lofs; nor did
he ever fail to mention her with refpect,
after his fentiments of things may have

been

been fuppofed, from greater commerce with the world, to have undergone a change.

His liberality with refpect to pecuniary concerns was early difplayed; and at no time of his life does he feem to have confidered money in any other light than as an inftrument of procuring happinefs to himfelf and others. The little fortune that his wife poffeffed he gave to her fifter; and during his refidence at Newington he beftowed much in charity, and made a handfome donation to the diffenting congregation there, for the purpofe of providing a dwelling-houfe for the minifter.

His attachment to religion was a principle imbibed from his earlieft years, which continued fteady and uniform

8   through

through life. The body of Chriftians to whom he particularly united himfelf were the Independents, and his fyftem of belief was that of the moderate Calvinifts. But though he feems early to have made up his mind as to the doctrines he thought beft founded, and the mode of worfhip he moft approved, yet religion abftractedly confidered, as the relation between man and his Maker, and the grand fupport of morality, appears to have been the principal object of his regard. He was lefs folicitous about modes and opinions, than the internal fpirit of piety and devotion; and in his eftimate of different religious focieties, the circumftances to which he principally attended, were their zeal and fincerity. As it is the nature of fects in

general,

general, to exhibit more earneſtneſs in
doctrine, and ſtrictneſs in diſcipline, than
the eſtabliſhment from which they diſ-
ſent, it is not to be wondered at that
a perſon of Mr. *Howard*'s diſpoſition
ſhould regard the various denominations
of ſectaries with predilection, and attach
himſelf to their moſt diſtinguiſhed members. In London he ſeems chiefly to
have joined the Baptiſt congregation in
Wild-ſtreet, long under the miniſtry of
the much-reſpected Dr. Stennett. His
connexions were, I believe, leaſt with
that claſs called the Rational Diſſenters;
yet he probably had not a more intimate
friend in the world than Dr. Price, who
always ranked among them. It was his
conſtant practice to join in the ſervice of
the eſtabliſhment when he had not the

7.   opportunity

opportunity of attending a place of diffenting worfhip; and though he was
warmly attached to the interefts of the
party he efpoufed, yet he had that true
fpirit of catholicifm, which led him to
honour virtue and religion wherever he
found them, and to regard the *means*
only as they were fubfervient to the *end*.

He was created a Fellow of the Royal
Society on May 13, 1756. This honour
was not, I prefume, conferred upon him
in confequence of any extraordinary proficiency in fcience which he had manifeft-
ed; but rather in conformity to the laudable practice of that fociety, of attaching
gentlemen of fortune and leifure to the
interefts of knowledge, by incorporat-
ing them into their body. Mr. *Howard*
was not unmindful of the obligation he

lay

lay under to contribute fomething to the common ftock of information.. Three fhort papers of his are publifhed in the *Tranfactions*. Thefe are,

In Vol. LIV. On the Degree of Cold obferved at Cardington in the Winter of 1763, when Bird's Thermometer was as low as 10½.

In Vol. LVII. On the Heat of the Waters at Bath, containing a Table of the Heat of the Waters of the different Baths.

In Vol. LXI. On the Heat of the Ground on Mount Vefuvius.

This lift may ferve to give an idea of the kind and degree of his philofophical refearch. Meteorological obfervations were much to his tafte; and even in his later tours, when he was occupied by

very

very different objects, he never travelled
without fome inftruments for that purpofe. I have heard him likewife mention fome experiments on the effects of
the union of the primary colours in different proportions, in which he employed himfelf with fome affiduity.

After the death of his wife, in the year
1756, he fet out upon another tour, ir.-
tending to commence it with a vifit to
the ruins of Lifbon. The event of this
defign will be hereafter mentioned. He
remained abroad a few months; and, on
his return, began to alter the houfe on
his eftate at Cardington near Bedford,
where he fettled. In 1758 he made a
very fuitable alliance with Mifs *Henrietta*
Leeds, eldeft daughter of Edward Leeds,
Efq; of Croxton, Cambridgefhire, king's

C 4   ferjeant;

ferjeant; and fifter of the prefent Edward Leeds, Efq; a Mafter in Chancery;
and of Jofeph Leeds, Efq; of Croydon.
With this lady, who poffeffed in an eminent degree all the mild and amiable
virtues proper to her fex, he paffed, as
I have often heard him declare, the only
years of true enjoyment which he had
known in life. Soon after his marriage
he purchafed Watcombe, in the New
Foreft, Hampfhire, and removed thither. Concerning his way of life in this
pleafant retreat, I find nothing characteriftic to relate, except the ftate of perfect fecurity and harmony in which he
managed to live in the midft of a people, againft whom his predeceffor thought
it neceffary to employ all the contrivances of engines and guns in order to

preferve

preferve himfelf from their hoftilities.
He had, indeed, none of thofe propen-
fities which fo frequently embroil country gentlemen with their neighbours,
both fmall and great. He was no fportf-
man, no executor of the game laws, and
in no refpect an encroacher on the rights
and advantages of others. In poffeffing
him, the poor could not fail foon to find
that they had acquired a protector and
benefactor; and I am unwilling to believe that in any part of the world thefe
relations are not returned with gratitude
and attachment. After continuing at
Watcombe three or four years, he fold
the place, and went back to Cardington,
which thenceforth became his fixed refidence.

Here

Here he steadily pursued those plans, both with respect to the regulation of his personal and family concerns, and to the promotion of the good of those around him, which principle and inclination led him to approve. Though without the ambition of making a splendid appearance, he had a taste for elegant neatness in his habitation and furniture. His sobriety of manners and peculiarities of living did not fit him for much promiscuous society; yet no man received his select friends with more true hospitality; and he always maintained an intercourse with several of the first persons in his county, who knew and respected his worth. Indeed, however uncomplying he might be with the free-

doms

doms and irregularities of polite life, he
was by no means negligent of its received forms; and, though he might be de-
nominated a man of fcruples and fingularities, no one would difpute his claim
to the title of a *gentleman*.

But the terms on which he held fociety with perfons of his own condition,
are of much lefs importance in the view
I mean to take of his character, than
the methods by which he rendered himfelf a blefling to the indigent and friend-
lefs in a fmall circle, before he extended
his benevolence to fo wide a compafs.
It feems to have been the capital object of his ambition, that the poor in his
village fhould be the moft orderly in
their manners, the neateft in their perfons and habitations, and poffeffed of the
greateft

greateft fhare of the comforts of life, that could be met with in any part of England. And as it was his difpofition to carry every thing he undertook to the greateft pitch of perfection, fo he fpared no pains or expence to effect this purpofe. He began by building a number of neat cottages on his eftate, annexing to each a little land for a garden, and other conveniences. In this project, which might be confidered as an object of tafte as well as of benevolence, he had the full concurrence of his excellent partner. I remember his relating, that once, having fettled his accounts at the clofe of a year, and found a balance in his favour, he propofed to his wife to make ufe of it in a journey to London, or any other gratification fhe chofe. " What a pretty

cottage

cottage it would build," was her anfwer; and the money was fo employed. Thefe comfortable habitations he peopled with the moft induftrious and fober tenants he could find; and over them he exercifed the fuperintendence of mafter and father combined. He was careful to furnifh them with employment, to affift them in ficknefs and diftrefs, and to educate their children. In order to preferve their morals, he made it a condition that they fhould regularly attend their feveral places of worfhip, and abftain from pub-lic-houfes, and from fuch amufements as he thought pernicious; and he fecur-ed their compliance with his rules by making them tenants at will.

I fhall here beg leave to digrefs a lit-tle, in order to make fome general ob-

fervations

fervations on the different methods that
may be propofed for bettering the condition of the loweft and moft numerous
clafs among us. In the ftate in which
they too frequently appear, depreffed to
the extremeft point of indigence, unable
by their utmoft exertions to obtain more
than the bare neceffaries of exiftence,
debafed by the total want of inftruction, and partaking of nothing that
can dignify the human character, it is
no wonder that a benevolent perfon of
the higher ranks in fociety fhould confider them as creatures of an inferior
fpecies, only to be benefited by the conftant exercife of his authority and fuperintendence. And I believe the fact to
be, that, from the operation of our poor
laws and other circumftances, the poor

in

in this country are more thoughtlefs, improvident, and helplefs, than thofe of almoft any other nation. Humanity will therefore, in fuch a ftate of things, think it neceffary to affume the entire management. of thofe who can neither think nor act for their own good; and will direct and over-rule all their concerns, juft as it would thofe of children and idiots. In fhort, it will aim at fuch a kind of influence, as the Jefuits of Paraguay eftablifhed, (perhaps with the fame benevolent views) over the fimple natives.

But is this ftate of pupilage to be perpetual? and, in a land of liberty and equal laws, is the great body of people always to exift in a condition of actual fubjection to and dependence on the few?

Are

Are they never to be intrufted with their own happinefs, but always to look up for fupport and direction to thofe who in reality are lefs independent than them-felves? This is an idea which a liberal mind will be unwilling to admit; and it will anxioufly look forward to a period, in which meannefs of condition fhall not neceffarily imply debafement of nature; but thofe of *every* rank in fociety, feeling powers within themfelves to fecure their effential comforts, fhall rely upon their own exertions, and be guided by the dictates of their own reafon. That this is not an imaginary ftate of things, the general condition of the loweft claffes in fome countries, and even in fome parts of England, where the working poor, at the fame time that their earn-

ings

ings enable them to procure the comforts of life, are inured to habits of sobriety and frugality, is a sufficient proof.

There are few counties in England which afford less employment to a numerous poor than that of Bedford; of course, wages are low, and much distress would prevail, were it not for the humanity of the gentlemen who reside upon their estates. Among these, Mr. *Howard* distinguished himself by a peculiar attention to the comfort and improvement of his dependents; and he was accordingly held by them in the highest respect and veneration. I may add, that he possessed their *love*; which is not always the case with those who render essential services to people of that class. But he treated them with kindness, as well as with be-

D   neficence;

neficence; and he particularly avoided
every thing ftern or imperious in his
manner towards them. Whatever there
might appear of ftrictnefs in the difcipline he enforced, it had only in view
their beft interefts; and if under his pro-
tection they could pafs a tranquil old
age in their own comfortable cottages,
rather than end their lives in a work-
houfe, the fubordination to which they
fubmitted was amply compenfated. It
is certain that the melioration of manners and principles which he promot-
ed, was the moft effectual means of
eventually rendering them more independent; and I have reafon to know,
that, latterly at leaft, he was as well affected to the *rights*, as he was folicitous
to augment the *comforts*, of the poor.

3   His

His charities were not confined to thofe more immediately connected with his property; they took in the whole circle of neighbourhood. His bounty was particularly directed to that fundamental point in improving the condition of the poor, giving them a fober and ufeful education. From early life he attended to this object; and he eftablifhed fchools for both fexes, conducted upon the moft judicious plan. The girls were taught reading, and needlework in a plain way: the boys reading, and fome of them writing, and the rudiments of arithmetic. They were regularly to attend public worfhip in the way their parents approved. The number brought up in thefe fchools was fluctuating, but the inftitutions were uninterrupted.

rupted. In every other way in which a
man thoroughly difpofed to do good
with the means providence has beftowed
upon him, can exercife his liberality,
Mr. *Howard* ftood among the foremoft..
He was not only a fubfcriber to various
public fchemes of benevolence, but his
private charities were largely diffufed,
and remarkably well directed. It was,
indeed, only to his particular confidents
and coadjutors that many of thefe were
ever known; but they render him the
moft ample teftimony in this refpect.
His very intimate and confidential friend,
the Rev. Mr. Thomas Smith of Bedford,
gives me the following account of this
part of his conduct, at a time when
he was deeply engaged in thofe public
exertions which might be fuppofed to

interfere

interfere with his private and local benefactions. " He ftill continued to
devife liberal things for his poor neighbours and tenants; and, confidering how
much his heart and time were engaged
in his great and comprehenfive plans,
it was furprifing with what minutenefs
he would fend home his directions about
his private donations. His *fchools* were
continued to the laft." It is impoffible any ftronger proof can be given,
that the habit of doing good was wrought
into his very nature, than that, while his
public actions placed him without a rival
for deeds of philanthropy, he fhould ftill
be unable to fatisfy his benevolent defires without his accuftomed benefits to
his neighbours and dependents.

D 3

Another

· Another early feature of that character which Mr. *Howard* afterwards so conspicuously displayed, was a determined resistance of injustice and oppression. No one could be more firmly relied on as the protector of right and innocence against unfeeling and unprincipled power. His indignation was roused by any attempts to encroach or domineer; and his spirit led him, without hesitation, to express, both in words and actions, his sense of such conduct. As no man could be more perfectly independent, both in mind and situation, than himself, he made that use of his advantage which every independent man ought to do;—he acted as principle directed him, regardless whom he might displease by it;

it; he strongly marked his different sensations with respect to different characters; and he was not less strenuous in
opposing pernicious schemes, than in
promoting beneficial ones.

The love of order and regularity likewife marked the early as well as the later
periods of his life; it directed his own
domestic concerns equally with his plans
for the benefit of others. His disposition
of time was exact and methodical. He
accurately knew the state of all his
affairs; and the hand of economy regulated what the heart of generosity dif-
penfed. His taste in dress, furniture, and
every thing exterior, was turned to sim-
plicity and neatness; and this conformity of disposition rendered him an ad-
mirer of the sect of Quakers, with many

individuals

individuals of which he maintained an intimate connexion.

In common with many other benevolent and virtuous characters, he had a fondnefs for gardening, and the cultivation of plants both ufeful and ornamental. Indeed, as his own diet was almoft entirely of the vegetable kind, he had various inducements to attend to this pleafing occupation. - That moft valuable root, the potato, was a great favourite with him; and a remarkably productive fpecies of it, which he recommended to public notice, was diftinguifhed by his name. His garden was an object of curiofity, both for the elegant manner in which it was laid out, and for the excellence of its productions; and in his various travels he frequently

brought

brought home, and distributed among his friends, the seeds of curious kinds of cultivated vegetables.

In this manner Mr. *Howard* passed the tranquil years of his settled residence at Cardington; happy in himself, and the instrument of good to all around him. But this state was not long to continue. His domestic felicity received a fatal wound from the death of his beloved wife, in the year 1765, soon after delivery of her only child. It is unnecessary to say how a heart like his must have felt on such an event. They who have been witnesses of the sensibility with which, many years afterwards, he recollected it, and know how he honoured and cherished her memory, will conceive his sensations at that trying period. He

was

was thenceforth attached to his home only by the duties annexed to it; of which the moſt intereſting was the education of his infant ſon. This was an office which almoſt immediately commenced; for, according to his ideas, education had place from the very firſt dawn of the mental faculties. The very unfortunate iſſue of his cares, with reſpect to his ſon, has cauſed a charge to be brought againſt him very deeply affecting his paternal character. That this charge was in its main circumſtance falſe and calumnious, has, I truſt, been proved, to the ſatisfaction of the public, by appeals to facts which have remained uncontroverted. I ſhall not, therefore, go over again the ground of this controverſy; but ſhall rather follow the pro-

per

per line of this work, by briefly diſplay-
ing Mr. *Howard*'s ideas on education,
and his manner of executing them.

Regarding children as creatures poſſeſſed of ſtrong paſſions and deſires, without reaſon and experience to controul
them, he thought that Nature ſeemed,
as it were, to mark them out as the
ſubjects of abſolute authority; and that
the firſt and fundamental principle to be
inculcated upon them, was implicit and
unlimited obedience. This cannot be
effected by any proceſs of *reaſoning*, before reaſon has its commencement; and
therefore muſt be the reſult of *coercion.*
Now, as no man ever more effectually
combined the *leniter in modo* with the
fortiter in re, the coercion he practiſed
was calm and gentle, but at the ſame
time

time steady and resolute. I shall give an
instance of it which I had from himself.
His child one day, wanting something
which he was not to have, fell into a fit
of crying, which the nurse could not
pacify. Mr. *Howard* took him from
her, and laid him quietly in his lap, till,
fatigued with crying, he became still.
This process, a few times repeated, had
such an effect, that the child, if crying
ever so violently, was rendered quiet
the instant his father took him. In a
similar manner, without harsh words and
threats, still less blows, he gained every
other point which he thought necessary
to gain, and brought the child to such a
habit of obedience, that I have heard
him say, he believed his son would have
put his finger into the fire if he had
commanded

commanded him. Certain it is, that many fathers could not, if they approved it, execute a plan of this kind; but Mr. *Howard* in this cafe only purfued the general method which he took to effect any thing which a thorough conviction of its propriety induced him to undertake. It is abfurd, therefore, to reprefent him as wanting that milk of human kindnefs for his only fon, with which he abounded for the reft of his fellow-creatures; for he aimed at what he thought the good of both, by the very fame means; and, if he carried the point further with refpect to his fon, it was only becaufe he was more interefted in his welfare. But this courfe of difcipline, whatever be thought of it, could not have been long practifed, fince the child

was

was early fent to fchool, and the father
lived very little at home afterwards.
As to its *effect* on the youth's mind (if
that, and not intention, be the circumftance on which Mr. *Howard*'s vindica-
cation is to depend), I confider it as a
manifeft impoffibility, that controuling
the *child*, fhould have been the caufe of
the *young man's* infanity. If any fuch
remote caufe could be fuppofed capable
of producing fuch an effect, the oppofite
extreme of indulgence would have been
a much more likely one. But I think it
highly probable, that a father, whofe
prefence was affociated with the percep-
tion of reftraint and refufal, fhould always
have infpired more awe than affection; and
fhould never have created that filial confidence, which is both the moft pleafing
and

and moſt ſalutary of the ſentiments attending that relation. And this has been
the great evil of that rigorous mode of
education, once ſo · general, and ſtill
frequent, among perſons of a particular
perſuaſion. I have authority to ſay, that
Mr. *Howard* was at length ſenſible that
he had in ſome meaſure miſtaken the
mode of forming his ſon to that character he wiſhed him to acquire ; though,
with reſpect to his mental derangement, I know that he imputed no
blame to himſelf on that head. With
what parental ſorrow he was affected by
that event will appear in the progreſs of
the narration.

. Having now given ſuch a view of the
temper and manners of this excellent
perſon, ·in his private ſituation, as may
ſerve

ferve to introduce him to the reader's
acquaintance at the time of his affuming
a public chara&ter, I fhall, without further delay, proceed to trace him through
thofe years of his life, the employment
of which alone has rendered him an ob-
je&t of the curiofity and admiration of
his countrymen.

In the year 1773 Mr. *Howard* was
nominated High-Sheriff of the county of
Bedford. An obftacle, however, lay in
the way of his accepting that office, concerning which I fhall take the liberty of
making a few remarks.

When a principled Diffenter, whofe
condition in life permits him to afpire
to the honour of ferving his country in
fome poft of magiftracy, reflects on his
fituation, he finds that he muft make

his

his election of one of the three following
determinations. He must either comply with a religious rite of another
church, merely on account of its being
made the condition of receiving the office;
or take upon himself the office without
such compliance, under all the hazard
that attends it; or he must quietly sit
down under that *vacation* from public
charges: which the state, in its wisdom,
has imposed upon him, satisfied with
promoting the welfare of individuals by
modes not interdicted to him. It would
be great presumption in me to decide
which of these determinations is most
conformable to duty. In fact, there is
only a choice of difficulties; and the de-
cision between them must be left to every
man's own feelings, which, if his inten-

E   tions

tions be good and honeſt, will ſcarcely lead him wrong. But it was perfectly ſuitable to Mr. *Howard*'s character to make option of *the office with the hazard:* for as, on the one hand, no conſideration on earth could have induced him to violate his religious principles; ſo, on the other, his active diſpoſition, and zeal for the public good, ſtrongly impelled him to aſſume a ſtation in which thoſe qualities might have free ſcope for exertion; and as to perſonal hazard, *that* was never an obſtacle in his way. There may be caſuiſts who will condemn this choice, and regard it as a ſerious offence againſt the laws of his country, to have taken upon him an office without complying with its preliminary conditions. But, I conceive, the ſincere philanthropiſt will

rather

rather make a different reflection, and feel a shock in thinking, that, had Mr. *Howard* been influenced by those apprehensions which would have operated upon most men, he would have been excluded from that situation, which gave occasion to all those services which he rendered to humanity in his own country, and throughout Europe *.

He

* The penalties to which Mr. *Howard* in this instance exposed himself are declared in the following clause of the *Test Act*, which cannot too often be placed before the eyes of Britons. " Every per-
" son that shall neglect or refuse to take the sacra-
" crament as aforesaid, and yet, after such neglect
" or refusal, shall execute any of the said offices or
" employments, and being thereupon lawfully con-
" victed, *shall be disabled to sue or use any action,*
" *bill, plaint, or information, in course of law, or to*
" *prosecute any suit in any court of equity, or to be*
" *guardian of any child, or executor or administrator*

" of

He entered upon his office with the re-
folution of performing all its duties with

" *of any perfon, or capable of any legacy or deed of*
" *gift, or to bear any office ; and fhall forfeit the fum*
" *of five hundred pounds, to be recovered by him or*
" *them that fhall fue for the fame.*"—In the debate
on the repeal of this act, the Mover with much eloquence introduced the very cafe of Mr. *Howard*,
and feemed confiderably to imprefs his audience by
the fuppofition of fuch a man fuffering its penalties,
in confequence of an information which any villain
might lay againft him. In reply it was faid, that,
whatever were a man's intentions, if he voluntarily
contravened a known law of his country, it ought
not to be reckoned a hardfhip that he incurred the
penalties by which it was fanctioned. And this rea-
foning is undoubtedly juft, as it refpects the intereft
of an individual put in competition with the fecurity
of a law. But furely it is a proper confideration
for the legiflature, whether a law be grounded on
thofe principles of equity and general utility which
can juftify the impofition of fuch dreadful penalties
for the breach of it, efpecially when experience has
fh wr, that the moft confcientious and well-inten-
tioned perfons are moft liable to incur them.

that

that punctuality which marked his conduct in every thing he undertook. Of
thefe, one of the moft important, though
leaft agreeable, is the infpection of the
prifons within its jurifdiction. But this
to him was not only an act of duty, it
interefted him as a material concern of
humanity.

The attention of Mr. *Howard* to perfons " fick and in prifon" is by himfelf
dated as far back as the year 1756, when
he was induced by a fingular, but what
I fhould call a fublime, curiofity to vifit
Lifbon, then lying in the recent ruins of its
terrible earthquake. The packet in which
he failed being taken by a French pri-
vateer, he, with the reft of the crew,
was firft expofed to all the barbarities
exercifed by thofe licenfed pirates, who

E 3   poffefs

poffefs the right of the fword, not mollified by the feelings of gentlemen; and, on his arrival in France, he for a time endured fome of the hardfhips of a prifoner of war, and became acquainted with all the fufferings of his countrymen in the fame fituation. Thefe, on his return to England, he took care to make known to the *Commiffioners of Sick and Wounded Seamen,* who gave him their thanks for his information, and exerted themfelves to obtain redrefs. It was impoffible that fo feeling a leffon of the calamities inflicted upon the unprotected claffes of mankind, by fellow-creatures " dreffed in a little brief authority," fhould fail to make a durable impreffion on fuch a mind as Mr. *Howard*'s.

It

It was not, however, till the period of his ferving the office of fheriff, that the diftreffes of thofe confined in the civil prifons of his own country engaged his particular notice. In the Introduction to his *State of the Prifons* he has, with the moft unaffuming fimplicity, related the gradual progrefs of his inquiries; and in what manner he was led, from an examination of the gaols in his own fmall county, to an inveftigation of all the circumftances belonging to this branch of police throughout the kingdom.

The firft thing which ftruck him, was the enormous injuftice of remanding to prifon for the payment of *fees*, thofe who had been acquitted or difcharged without trial. As the magiftrates of his county, though willing to redrefs this

grievance,

grievance, did not conceive themſelves poſſeſſed of the power of granting a remedy, Mr. *Howard* travelled into ſome of the neighbouring counties in ſearch of a precedent. In this ſearch, ſcenes of calamity and injuſtice ſtill opening upon him, he went on, and paid viſits to moſt of the *County Gaols* in England. Some peculiarly deplorable objects coming in his view who had been brought from the *Bridewels*, he was induced to enter upon an examination of theſe places of confinement; for which purpoſe he travelled again into the counties he had before ſeen, and into all the reſt, viſiting *Houſes of Correction, City and Town Gaols.*

He had carried on theſe inquiries with ſo much aſſiduity, that ſo early as March 1774 he was deſired to communicate his
information

information to the Houſe of Commons, and received their thanks. As he was then little known, I cannot much wonder that ſo extraordinary an inſtance of pure and active benevolence was not univerſally comprehended, even by that patriotic body; for a member thought fit to aſk him, " at whoſe expence he travelled?" a queſtion which Mr. *Howard* could ſcarcely anſwer without ſome indignant emotions. Soon after this public teſtimony given to the exiſtence of great abuſes and defects in our priſons, a very worthy member, Mr. *Popham*, brought into the Houſe two bills, one *for the relief of acquitted priſoners in matter of fees*; the other, *for preſerving the health of priſoners.* Theſe ſalutary acts paſſed during the ſame ſeſſion, and

made

made a commencement of those reforms which have since been so much extended. Mr. *Howard*, aware of the great deficiency of the mode of *promulgating laws* among us, had these acts printed in a different character, and sent to every keeper of a county gaol in England.

.. In this year he was induced, by the urgent persuasions of his neighbours and friends of the town of Bedford, to stand candidate, in conjunction with Mr. *Whitbread*, to represent that borough in Parliament. No two persons could be better entitled to the esteem of a town; and they were very warmly supported in a contest, which however terminated in the return of two other gentlemen. Mr. *Whitbread* and Mr. *Howard* petitioned the House against the return; and the

event

event was, that the former, and one of
the fitting members, were declared duly
elected. To thofe who are acquainted
with the conftitution of that borough, it
will not appear extraordinary, that a perfon poffeffing the attachment of a ma-
jority of the inhabitant voters fhould lofe
his election. This, however, was a moft
fortunate circumftance for the public;
fince, if Mr. *Howard* had obtained a
feat in the Houfe of Commons, his plans
for the reformation of prifons muft have
been brought within a narrow compafs; and the collateral inquiries which,
fo greatly to the advantage of humanity,
he afterwards adopted, could never have
exifted.

It was Mr. *Howard*'s intention to have
publifhed his account of Englifh Prifons

in

in fpring 1775; but as he was fenfible,
that to point out defects, without at the
fame time fuggefting remedies, would be
of little advantage, he thought it beft to
examine with his own eyes what had
been actually put in practice with refpect
to this part of police, in fome of the moft
enlightened countries on the continent.
Accordingly, in that year he vifited France,
Flanders, Holland, and Germany; and
in 1776 repeated his vifit to thofe countries, and alfo went to Switzerland. In
the intervals he made a journey to Scotland and Ireland, and revifited the county gaols and many others in England.

Thus furnifhed with a ftock of information greater than had ever before
been collected on this fubject; and, indeed, probably greater than *any* man
had,

had, in the fame fpace of time, ever collected on *any* fubject that required fimilar pains; he offered it to the public in
1777, in a quarto volume of near 500
pages, dedicated to the Houfe of Commons, by way of grateful acknowledgment for the honour conferred on him
by their thanks, and for the attention
they had beftowed on the bufinefs. Before I proceed to give an account of this
work, I fhall juft obferve, that fo zealous
was Mr. *Howard* to diffufe information,
and fo determined to obviate any idea
that he meant to repay his expences by
the profitable trade of *book-making*, that,
befides a profufe munificence in prefenting
copies to all the principal perfons in the
kingdom, and all his particular friends,
he infifted on fixing the price of the vo-

7   lume

lume fo low, that, had every copy been
fold, he would ftill have prefented the
public with all the plates, and great part
of the printing. And this practice he
followed in all his fubfequent publications; fo that, with literal propriety, he
may be faid to have *given* them to the
world. By the large expences of his
journey, charities, and publications, he
has made himfelf even a greater *pecuniary*
benefactor to mankind than can readily
be paralleled in any age or country, his
proportionate circumftances confidered.
Yet how fmall a part was this of the fa-
crifices he made!

He chofe the prefs of Mr. Eyres at
Warrington, induced by various elegant
fpecimens which had iffued from it, and
by the opportunity a country prefs af-

8   forded,

forded, of having the work done under his own infpection, at his own time, and with all the minute accuracy of correction he determined to beftow on it. I may alfo fay, that an opinion of the advantage he might there enjoy of fome literary affiftance in the revifion and improvement of his papers, was a farther motive. To this choice I was indebted for that intimate perfonal acquaintance with him, which I fhall ever efteem one of the moft honourable circumftances of my life, and the lively recollection of which will, I truft, never quit me while memory remains. He refided in Warrington during the whole time of printing, and his attention to bufinefs was moft indefatigable. During a very fevere winter he made it his practice to rife at

three

three or four in the morning, for the purpofe of collating every word and fi-gure of his daily proof fheet with the original.

As I thought it right to mention Mr. *Howard*'s literary deficiencies, it is be-come neceffary to inform the public of the manner in which his works were com-pofed. On his return from his tours he took all his memorandum-books to an old retired friend of his, who affifted him in methodizing them, and copied out the whole matter in correct language. They were then put into the hands of Dr. *Price*, from whom they underwent a revifion, and received occafionally con-fiderable alterations. What Mr. *Howard* himfelf thought of the advantages they derived from his affiftance, will appear

from

from the following paffages in letters to
Dr. Price. " I am afhamed to think
" how much I have accumulated your
" labours, yet I glory in that affiftance
" to which I owe fo much credit in the
" world, and, under Providence, fuccefs
" in my endeavours."——" It is from
" your kind aid and affiftance, my dear
" friend, that I derive fo much of my
" character and influence. I exult in
" declaring it, and fhall carry a grate-
" ful fenfe of it to the laft hour of my
" exiftence."—With his papers thus corrected, Mr. *Howard* came to the prefs at
Warrington; and firft he read them all
over carefully with me, which perufal
was repeated, fheet by fheet, as they
were printed. As new facts and obfervations were continually fuggefting

F themfelves

themfelves to his mind, he put the matter of them upon paper as they occurred, and then requefted me to clothe them in fuch expreffions as I thought proper. On thefe occafions, fuch was his diffidence, that I found it difficult to make him acquiefce in his own language when, as frequently happened, it was unexceptionable. Of this additional matter, fome was interwoven with the text, but the greater part was neceffarily thrown into notes, which, in fome of his volumes, are numerous.

The title of this firft work is, *The State of the Prifons in England and Wales; with preliminary Obfervations, and an Account of fome Foreign Prifons.* It begins with *a general View of Diftrefs in Prifons,* fhewing in what refpects thofe of England

land are deficient in the articles of food, water, bedding, and freſh air; and that the morals of the priſoners are totally neglected, the moſt criminal and abandoned being ſuffered to corrupt the younger and leſs practiſed. Notice is alſo taken of the *gaol-fever*, a diſeaſe which has in a peculiar manner infeſted the priſons of this country, and has at various times ſpread its ravages from them among our courts of judicature, our fleets, and armies. The author's next ſection is on *Bad Cuſtoms in Priſons*, under which he takes notice of the demand of garniſh, the permiſſion of gaming, the uſe of irons, the practice of varying the towns where the aſſizes are held, the local unfrequency of gaol-delivery, the fees ſtill demanded by clerks

F 2　　　　　　of

of affize and of the peace, the non-refi-
dency of gaolers, the crowding of. gaols
with the wives and children of prifoners,
and the circumftance of fome gaols being
private property. From this, and the
foregoing fection, every one muft be
convinced of the dreadful ftate of our
police in this important matter, and the
abfolute neceffity for a reformation. For
proof that the complaints here made in
general terms are not unfounded or ex-
aggerated, he properly refers to the fubfequent account of particular gaols, where
they are too abundantly verified. He
concludes the fecond fection with an enumeration of all the prifoners in England
and Wales, under their feveral claffes,
who, in 1776, amounted to 4084, a
number much lefs than fome vague con-
jectures

jectures had ftated, yet fufficiently great to demand the ferious attention of the legiflature, efpecially when it is confidered that every man in prifon may be reckoned to have two dependents on him for fupport.

Mr. *Howard*'s third fection offers *propofed Improvements in the Structure and Management of Prifons.* He begins with obfervations on the prifon itfelf, with refpect to its fituation and plan, the latter of which is illuftrated by an engraving. He then proceeds to that moft effential topic, the regulations. Thefe he confiders under the feveral heads of gaoler, chaplain, furgeon, fees, cleanlinefs, food, bedding, rules and orders, and infpector. He much infifts upon the neceffity of abfolutely taking away the

F 3

tap from the keepers of prisons, the poffeffion of which was obvioufly the caufe
of promoting intemperance and riot,
from the intereft it gave the keeper in
fuch irregularities. In lieu of this fource
of profit, he propofes a liberal addition to
the falaries of this officer, the importance
and refpectability of whofe employ he
every where inculcates. He makes a feparate article of bridewels, the original
penitentiary-houfes of the country, and
planned with much wifdom, but which,
by long neglect and abufe, were become
rather a nuifance than an advantage to
the police. In many of them, though
the perfons confined were fentenced to
hard labour, no work of any kind was
done; and this ftate of idlenefs, with the
company of hardened criminals, proved

to

to be a moſt effeſtual method of complet-
ing the corruption of young and petty offenders. Various excellent remarks and
ſuggeſtions are given in the whole of this
ſeſtion, which contains the ground-work
of all improvement in the economy of
priſons and houſes of correſtion.

In ſeſt. IV. Mr. *Howard* gives an account of *Foreign Priſons*; not of *all* he
had ſeen, but of ſuch only as afforded
matter of inſtruſtion; nor in theſe does
he notice the frauds and defeſts he obſerved, for he ſays, " the redreſs and
" inveſtigation of *foreign* abuſes was not
" my objeſt." The countries of which
the priſons are deſcribed are France,
Switzerland, Germany, Holland, and
Flanders. In the firſt, the ſuſpicious
policy which *then* prevailed would have

F 4 rendered

rendered it very difficult for him to have obtained accefs to the interior part of the prifons, had he not availed himfelf of a benevolent rule, which permits any per- fon to diftribute *alms* to the prifoners with his own hands. A fpirit of order and precifion, tempered with humanity, was obfervable in the conduct of this department, the regulations of which were fixed by a very comprehenfive and judicious code contained in an *arret* of 1717. In *Switzerland*, the feparation of male and female prifoners, the folitary confinement of felons, and the employ- ment of thofe called galley-flaves, are circumftances deferving notice. The *German* prifons are regulated in a fimilar manner; and the houfes of correction at *Manheim*, *Hamburgh*, and *Bremen*, af-

ford

ford ufeful examples of order and induftry. But it is in *Holland* that the purpofe of reforming criminals by a courfe
of difcipline is carried into execution with
moft care and effect. Few debtors and
few atrocious offenders are to be found
there; and the rafp and fpin-houfes contain the great body of prifoners. The
regulations of thefe are given in detail,
and the different employments of the
prifoners in different towns are particularly noted. Holland appears to be Mr.
Howard's great fchool, to which we fhall
fee that he was never wearied in returning. The *Auftrian Netherlands* offer fome
of the largeft eftablifhments of the penitentiary kind, and prove the poffibility
of managing a great number of criminals
fo as to make them ufeful to the ftate,

and

and decent in their behaviour, by the aid
of steady difcipline and feparate confinement at night. Mr. *Howard* faw, what
I fuppofe was then deemed an impoffibility in England, in the houfe of correction at *Ghent*, near 190 ftout criminals governed with as much apparent
eafe as the moft fober and well-difpofed
affembly in civil fociety. The regulations of this prifon are defervedly given
at fome length. Mr. *Howard* concludes
this fection with a forcible and manly
appeal to his countrymen with refpect to
the comparifon he was obliged to exhibit
between foreign and Englifh police in
this point, fo unfavourable to the latter;
calling upon his reader to judge, from
the facts laid before him, " whether a
defign of reforming our prifons be merely
visionary;

viſionary; and whether idleneſs, debau-
chery, diſeaſe, and famine, be the neceſ-
ſary attendants of a priſon, or only connected with it in our ideas, for want of
a more perfect knowledge and more enlarged views."

Section V. takes up the greateſt part of
the book. It contains a *particular account of Engliſh priſons*, arranged according to the circuits, and compriſing
every county in England and Wales.
The mode adopted is very well contrived
for the eaſy conſultation of magiſtrates and
other perſons concerned. Every principal
priſon in London, and every county and
city gaol, has the leading facts reſpecting
it diſpoſed in a ſhort table under the four
heads of *gaoler, priſoners, chaplain*, and
ſurgeon. A brief deſcription follows of
fituation,

fituation, plan, meafurements, &c. with fuch remarks, either of approbation or cenfure, as the circumftances fuggefted. Lifts are given of legacies and benefactions; and all tables of fees, and rules and orders, are copied *verbatim*. Next to thefe, are concife accounts of all the county bridewels, and the town gaols and bridewels, with occafional remarks. The work is clofed by fome *tables* relative to fees and numbers, crimes and punifhments of criminals. A fhort *conclufion* terminates the whole, in which the author apologizes for the language of cenfure he has fo often been compelled to ufe, enumerates the leading objects requiring reform, and promifes, that if fuch a *thorough parliamentary enquiry* into this great object, as alone can prove effectual

to

to put it upon a proper footing, fhould be undertaken, he would devote his time to a·more extenfive foreign journey, for the fake of obtaining new information to lay before the public.

I cannot difmifs the account of Mr. *Howard*'s firft and great work, without a few reflections, to which the contemplation of it gives rife. And firft, we may derive from it a clear idea of the capital objects which the author had at heart refpecting prifoners. Thefe were, to *alleviate their miferies*, and *correct their vices*. As to the former purpofe, he confidered that men, partaking a common nature, have certain claims upon their fellow-creatures which nothing can entirely abrogate;—that even the higheft degree of criminality does not abfolutely exclude

compaffion

compaſſion towards the perpetrators of crimes, eſpecially when ſuffering under their effects ;—that as no man paſſes through life without ſome deviation from ſtrict rectitude, ſo none has lived without the performance of ſome good actions ;— and that, although human laws muſt draw a line between ſuch circumſtances of conduct as do, or do not, come within their cognizance, yet there is a tribunal before which all mankind muſt appear as culprits, only diſtinguiſhed by the *degree* of delinquency. He further conſidered, that among the inmates of a priſon there is every poſſible degree of moral demerit, from the mere inconſiderate vio-lation of ſome hard, ill-underſtood, local law, to the deliberate breach of the moſt ſacred and univerſal rule of action ; and

that

that a great number are, in the eye of the law, innocent perfons, only under a temporary ftate of confinement, till their conduct is properly inveftigated. From thefe different views of the fubject, he convinced himfelf, that it was the duty of every fociety to pay due attention to the *health*, and, in fome degree, even to the *comforts*, of *all* who are held in a ftate of confinement;—that wanton and unneceffary rigour fhould be practifed upon *none*;—and that *fome* were entitled to all the indulgences compatible with their condition. It was, however, by no means his wifh (as fome chofe to reprefent it) to render a prifon fo comfortable an abode, that the loweft order of fociety might find their condition even bettered by admiffion into it. On the

4   contrary,

contrary, the fyftem of *difcipline* which he defired to.eftablifh, was fuch as would appear extremely grievous to thofe of an idle and licentious difpofition. For, whenever imprifonment was made. the *punifh-ment* of a crime, his idea of *reformation* became a leading principle in the regulation of prifons; and it was that which coft him the chief labour in collecting and applying facts. To accomplifh this end, he fhewed that thefe things were effential;—ftrict and conftant fuperintendence—clofe and regular employment—religious inftruction—rewards for induftry and good behaviour, and penalties for floth and audacioufnefs—diftribution into claffes and divifions according to age, fex, delinquency, &c.—and occafional and nocturnal folitude. In laying

down

down thefe regulations, he might be
thought to have given way to a certain
aufterity, were it not fo tempered by attention to the real demands of human
nature, and fanctified by a regard to the
beft interefts of offenders themfelves, that
the *friend of mankind* was ever apparent,
even in the ftrict difciplinarian. He extremely lamented that the plan of *reformation* feemed, of all parts of his fyftem
of improvement, leaft entered into or un-
derftood in this country. The vulgar
idea that our criminals are hardened
and abandoned beyond all poffibility of
amendment, appeared to him equally ir-
rational and pernicious. He fcorned,
through negligence or defpair, to give up
the worft cafes of mental corruption ; he
fully believed that proper remedies, duly

adminiftered,

administered, would recover a large share
of them ; and he thought it the greatest
of cruelties to consign a soul to perdition,
without having made every effort for re-
trieving it. Merely to *get rid* of convicts
by execution or perpetual banishment, he
regarded as a piece of barbarous policy,
equally denoting want of feeling, and
deficiency of resource ; and he had not
so much English prejudice about him, as
to suppose, that a system not adopted in
this country was therefore absurd or im-
practicable.

My second topic of reflection is the
striking proof this work affords of the
extensive benefit, arising from a *free
press*. By its means we see an individual,
enjoying neither royal nor ministerial,
patronage, but solely borne up by ardent

8   zeal

zeal for the public good, and the refources of his own mind and fortune, enabled, not only to lay before the world
complete information concerning a moft
important and little known fubject, but,
in fome meafure, alfo to *enforce* the correction of abufes, by bringing before *the
bar of the public* thofe by whofe negligence or criminality they had been fof-
tered. For as the hiftory of mankind has
fhewn, on the one hand, that palpable
injuftice and mifmanagement, even in an
abfolute government, cannot long ftand
their ground againft the odium of an enlightened public; fo, on the other, it has
proved, that even in free conftitutions,
notwithftanding all their boafted checks
and balances, very grofs abufes may long
prevail, unlefs they are placed in open

G 2   day,

day, and fubmitted to the cenfure of the
nation at large. It is fcarcely, I think,
to be doubted, that the freedom we enjoy
in this country, and the ultimate defeat
of every pernicious projeɑ̃, are lefs owing
to the *mechanifm* of our conftitution, than
to the habitual praɑ̃tice (rather affumed
by the fpirit of the people than granted
by the laws) of fubjeɑ̃ting every public
meafure to popular difcuffion by means
of the prefs. From this ready communication of faɑ̃ts and opinions, it has happened, that many ufeful defigns and improvements have among us originated
from perfons who had neither power nor
intereft of their own, but whofe plans
were adopted in confequence of the public conviɑ̃tion. The refpeɑ̃t paid to Mr.
Howard's virtues, abilities, and induftry,

placed

placed him in a manner at the head of the department in which he had engaged as a volunteer; and this, not only in his own country, but afterwards, in some meafure, throughout Europe. Though in exercifing the office of a cenfor he was fuperior to the fear of giving offence, yet he ever obferved the utmoft delicacy in marking out *individuals* as objects of blame. He boldly and forcibly difplayed the *abufe*, but left it to thofe more immediately concerned, to take notice of the *delinquent*. It cannot be queftioned, that numbers looked with an evil eye upon his keen refearches and free detections; but how could they venture, before the public, to confront a man whofe affertions were correct, whofe intentions were above all fufpicion, and

whofe

whofe life would ftand the fevereft teft ?
May this example animate all future
friends of mankind with a noble confidence becoming their caufe!

The Houfe of Commons now took up,
with laudable zeal, the important bufinefs of
regulating the prifons; and in the draught
of a bill " to punifh by imprifonment and
hard labour certain offenders, and to
eftablifh proper places for their reception," the plan was formed upon the
Rafp and Spin-houfes in Holland. Mr.
Howard was now called upon by his
promife, as well as his inclination, to
make a new tour for the purpofe of
acquiring frefh and more exact information. He, accordingly, in April 1778,
went over to *Holland,* and revifited with
the greateft attention the well-conducted
eftablifhments

eftablifhments of the penitentiary kind in the United Provinces. Thence he travelled into *Germany*, taking his courfe through Hanover and Berlin, to Vienna. From this capital he proceeded to *Italy* by Venice; and, having gone as far fouth as Naples, returned by the weftern fide of that country to *Switzerland*. Thence he purfued the courfe of the Rhine through *Germany*; and, croffing the *Low Countries* to *France*, returned to England in Jan. 1779. During the fpring and fummer of this year he made another complete tour of *England* and *Wales*, and like-wife took a journey through *Scotland* and *Ireland*.

The labours of thefe two years were certainly not lefs productive of ufeful information than his former journies. In

fome

some respects they were more valuable, since, being now fully master of his subject, and acquainted with the means of procuring the best intelligence, he pursued his inquiries with greater ease and effect. He was now, too, a distinguished character in Europe, and might venture to assume that kind of *authority*, to which the collection of facts, interesting to all civilized nations, seemed to entitle him. It is here proper to mention, that although he often found it necessary, especially when treading new ground, to avail himself of recommendations to persons high in rank and office; yet that he much preferred, when he could practise it, carrying on his researches as an unknown individual, whose business was not suspected, and who took such times and opportunities.

tunities of making his vifits, as secured him againſt any thing like difguife or preparation. And it was his general cuſtom, after he had once obtained acceſs to a priſon by the preſence and interpoſition of authority, to ſtay ſome time in the place, or revifit it, for the purpoſe of renewing his enquiries ſingle and unexpected. Thus careful was he to guard againſt deception; and with ſuch coolneſs of inveſtigation did he execute a deſign which it required ſo much ardour of mind to conceive!

I ſhall not, however, conceal, that ſome ſenſible and not uncandid obſervers of his conduct have thought him too apt to be prejudiced by firſt impreſſions, the effects of which it appeared extremely difficult to remove; and they have alſo

charged

charged him with fometimes giving un-
due credit to perfons of inferior condition,
at the places where he was making his
inquiries; and likewife with being apparently better pleafed with finding occafion to cenfure than to commend. If,
in a few inftances, there may have been
grounds for thefe imputations (as nothing
human is without its defects), yet I think
his works may, on the whole, be confi-
dently referred to, as proving, by an immenfe mafs of allowed and uncontradicted
facts, the accuracy of his reprefentations.
It is likewife to be confidered, that, as
abufes in general proceed from *fuperiors,*
it was not likely that a fair account of
them fhould be obtained from that quar-
ter: and, as his great purpofe was to *cor-*
rect, it is natural that his attention fhould

have

have been more drawn to what was wrong
than what was right. A Hercules who
went about in order to contend with
monfters, had little to do with the fair
forms of civil life. Yet numerous inftances of liberal praife may be found in
his works, efpecially where he could propofe the object of it as an example proper for imitation.

The tours now before us were likewife rendered richer in utility by the
comprehenfion of another great object,
that of *hofpitals.* To thefe inftitutions
of humanity Mr. *Howard* had long been
attached; he had been a promoter of
them, and attentive to their improvement; and in his journies through this
kingdom, he had feldom failed to vifit
the hofpitals and infirmaries fituated in

our

our principal towns. He had alfo, in his firft publication, taken curfory notice of a few which he faw abroad. But he now made them an avowed object of his examination; a circumftance, it may be fuppofed, not a little pleafing to his medical friends. For, although the knowledge collected by a profeffional man with fimilar opportunities would, doubtlefs, have been more applicable to the purpofe of fcience, yet matter of fact, accurately ftated by a fenfible obferver, muft ever have its value. Befides, where can we expect to fee the fpirit and qualities of a *Howard*, united, in one of our profeffion, with his fortune and leifure?

The fruit of all this refearch appeared in the year 1780, in an *Appendix to the State of the Prifons in England and Wales*;

containing

containing a further Account of Foreign Prifons and Hofpitals, with additional Remarks on the Prifons of this Country. It is a quarto volume of about 200 pages, with feveral plates. The work begins with the foreign prifons and hofpitals; and *Holland* takes the lead, fince a main object of the journey was a minute account of the excellent regulations of the houfes of correction in that country. Many of the rules, dietaries, &c. are copied; and on quitting the country, Mr. *Howard* gives his teftimony to the large field of information on this fubject that it affords, and fays, that he knows not which moft to admire, " the neatnefs and cleanlinefs appearing in the prifons, the induftry and regular conduct of the prifoners, or the humanity and at-

tention

tention of the magiſtrates and governors."
He takes little notice of the hoſpitals for
the ſick in Holland, not approving their
mode of keeping patients ſo warm, and
excluding the freſh air. At *Berlin*, the
regularity and ſtrictneſs of the police ſhews
the ruling ſpirit of the great Frederic.
A work-houſe here is conducted in the
beſt Dutch mode. *Vienna* affords little
to commend in its priſons: on the contrary, its horrid dungeons ſeem the
abode of the extremeſt human miſery.
Scarcely any thing in Mr. *Howard*'s de-
ſcriptions is more touching than the following picture: " In one of the dark
dungeons, down twenty-four ſteps, I
thought I had found a perſon with the
gaol-fever. He was loaded with heavy
irons, and chained to the wall: anguiſh

and

and mifery appeared with tears clotted on his face. He was not capable of fpeaking to me; but, on examining his breaft and feet for *petechiæ*, or fpots, and finding a ftrong intermitting pulfe, I was convinced that he was not ill of that diforder. A prifoner in an oppofite cell told me, that the poor creature had defired him to call for affiftance, and he had done it, but was not heard *." The

charities

---

* This fcene is the fubject of the frontifpiece to *Mr. Hayley's Ode to Mr. Howard*; and it is better drawn in the following ftanza of that performance.

Where in the dungeon's loathfome fhade
The fpeechlefs captive clanks his chain,
With heartlefs hope to raife that aid
His feeble cries have call'd in vain:
Thine eye his dumb complaint explores;
Thy voice his parting breath reftores;

Thy

charities of this city, chiefly founded by the late Emprefs Queen, are much more pleafing fubjects of defcription.

Mr. *Howard* entered *Italy* with high expectations of improvement from its numerous charitable inftitutions and public edifices; nor does it appear that he was altogether difappointed, as this country affords him a pretty long and interefting article. The governments in which a fpirit of improvement, and attention to public objects, feem moft to prevail, are thofe of Milan and Tufcany. The hofpitals in Italy afford fome novelties and ufeful hints; but there appears to be a great difference among them as to cleanlinefs and good management. *Rome* and

Thy cares his ghaftly vifage clear
From death's chill dew, with many a clotted tear,
And to his thankful foul returning life endear.

Milan

Milan have well conducted houfes of correction, of which plans and defcriptions are given. In a room of the former is infcribed a fentence, which fo admirably expreffed Mr. *Howard*'s idea concerning the purpofe of civil policy relative to criminals, that he would, I believe, almoft have thought it worth while to have travelled thither for that alone. PARUM EST COERCERE IMPROBOS POENA, NISI PROBOS EFFICIAS DISCIPLINA. *It is doing little to reftrain the bad by punifhment, unlefs you render them good by difcipline.* The *galleys* belonging to various ftates in Italy, and ufed for punifhment, may be ufefully compared with our *hulks*.

The weftern fide of *Germany* offers fome good regulations in its houfes of correction; but in general, the police of

this

this country is no object of imitation. The dungeons of *Liege* prefent pictures to the imagination more dreadful, if poffible, than thofe of Vienna. " In defcending deep below ground (fays Mr. *Howard)* I heard the moans of the miferable wretches in the dark dungeons. The fides and roof were all ftone. In wet feafons, water from the foffes gets into them, and has greatly damaged the floors."————" The dungeons in the *new* prifon are abodes of mifery ftill more fhocking; and confinement in them fo overpowers human nature, as fometimes irrecoverably to take away the fenfes. *I heard the cries of the diftracted* as I went down to them." Surely the Liegois cannot be blamed for endeavouring to place civil authority in different hands from

thofe

thofe who thus outraged the feelings of human nature!

The additional notices of *France* are diftinguifhed by an account of the Baftille, extracted from a fcarce pamphlet, which Mr. *Howard* procured, not without hazard, and a tranflation of the whole of which he likewife printed. He had reafon to believe, that this expofure to all Europe of the horrid fecrets of this " prifon houfe," was a caufe that his after-vifits to that country were attended with no fmall danger to his liberty; and it was once not improbable, that Mr. *Howard* fhould have been in the number of thofe victims whom the demolition of that fortrefs of defpotifm reftored to light and freedom. What a triumph muft it have been to him, to have learn-

ed,

ed, that the frowning towers, which could not be approached, or even gazed at, without offence, were levelled to the ground, as the firſt ſacrifice to the re-covered rights of a generous nation! It is remarkable, that France was of all countries that in which he found in-telligence concerning the priſons, and other government eſtabliſhments, moſt difficult to be obtained; and this union of the ſuſpicious rigour of the police with the exterior gaiety and frivolity of the national character, gave him no ſmall diſguſt. It is to be preſumed, that the change in their conſtitution will ſoften this contraſt into a deſirable harmony be-tween the principles of the adminiſtra-tion and the manners of the people.

Great Britain being then at war with
France,

France, Spain, and America, Mr. *Howard* could not be unmindful of that clafs of honourable prifoners to which he himfelf had once belonged. He very attentively vifited the Englifh prifoners of war confined in Calais and French Flanders, noting down their complaints, and all the particulars of their treatment. He alfo, as I have been well informed, clothed, at his own expence, feveral who had been fhipwrecked on the French coaft in the dreadful ftorm of December 31, 1778, and were left almoft naked. He likewife exerted himfelf in diffuading the men from enlifting with the French, who were endeavouring to feduce them; by which he greatly offended the perfons in office there, who could not imagine that he acted in all this as a private man, but

H 3

were

were ftrongly perfuaded that he was a fecret agent or fpy of the Englifh government. This natural fuppofition may ferve as fome apology for the fufpicion and illiberality with which he was conftantly treated in that country.

On his return to England, with the true fpirit of a citizen of the world, he paid immediate vifits to the French, Spanifh, and American prifoners of war in this country; nor did he forget thofe in Scotland and Ireland. The refults of his obfervations, given with the moft perfect impartiality, fucceed the account of foreign prifons and hofpitals; and it cannot be doubted that they had confiderable effect in alleviating the unavoidable hardfhips of war.

Mr. *Howard* next gives a brief account

of

of what he obferved worthy of notice in
his tours through *Scotland* and *Ireland*.
The former country being governed by
a different fyftem of municipal law from
that of England, affords fome ufeful remarks concerning imprifonment for debt,
the form of adminiftering an oath, and
the mode of conducting executions. *Ireland*, has not been at all behindhand
with the fifter kingdom in paffing acts
for the liberal improvement of its prifons;
but there did not at that time appear an
equal attention in magiftrates to put
them in execution. Some remarks here
introduced, concerning the practice of re-
cruiting the army out of the gaols, will
be thought important by thofe, who wifh
that the clafs of *armed citizens* fhould be

refpectable,

refpectable, in proportion to its confequence.

The next article relates to the *Hulks
on the Thames.* Thefe, at their firft inftitution, had been extremely unhealthy,
in confequence of faults which Mr. *Howard* pointed out in his former work.
Their ftate was now much mended by
means of parliamentary interference; yet,
on the whole, it was not a mode of imprifonment and employment which met
with his approbation. Some further remarks on the *Gaol-fever* fucceed; which,
in addition to the general caufes of want
of frefh air and cleanlinefs, he attributes
to fuch a fudden change of diet and
lodging as breaks the fpirits of convicts.
This correfponds with the medical doctrine

trine of the effect of *debilitating caufes*, in producing fevers of the *typhus* kind; yet it feems fuch a caufe as cannot well be avoided.

The remainder of the book is occupied by a frefh furvey of the prifons in England and Wales, in which fuch changes as had taken place fince his former publication are noted, with occafional obfervations. The reader will remark with pleafure, that in moft parts of the kingdom, various ufeful alterations had been made fince the period in which Mr. *Howard* began his inquiries; and the great fhare he had in occafioning them will be univerfally admitted.

His *conclufion* expreffes fatisfaction with the refult of his labours; and mentions, that it had been his intention now to re-

3   tire

tire to the tranquil enjoyment of that compe ence Providence had beſtowed on him, but that the earneſt perſuaſions of tloſe who thought him a proper perſon to ſuperintend one of the great plans he had ſo much recommended, had induced him ſtill to devote his time to the public. Concerning this matter, it is proper to enter into an explanation. I ſhall only firſt mention, that, together with this Appendix, there was printed a new edition, in octavo, of the *State of the Priſons*, with which all this additional matter was interwoven.

An act for eſtabliſhing *Penitentiary Houſes*, on which much labour and thought had been beſtowed by men of great ability, paſſed in 1779. By this act, three *ſuperviſors* were appointed for the

the purpofe of fuperintending the execution of the buildings. The whole kingdom would naturally turn its eyes on Mr.
Howard, as the firft perfon whofe fervices
fhould be engaged on this occafion; but
it was not an eafy tafk to obtain his ac-
quiefcence. Among other objections,
his extreme delicacy, with refpect to pecuniary emolument, ftood in his way; and
even the moderate falary annexed to this
office, feemed to him fcarcely compatible
with the abfolute difintereftednefs of conduct he had maintained, and was determined to preferve, during the whole of
his labours. At length, however, the
folicitations of his friends, particularly
of the late Sir W. Blackftone, the great
promoter of the defign, together with a
confcioufnefs of the fervice he might
render

render the public in this station, over-
came his reluctance. Having resolved
to accept of no salary for himself, and
having made the association of his highly-
respected friend, Dr. Fothergill, a condition of his compliance, he, with the
Doctor, and Mr. Whately, treasurer of the
Foundling-hospital, were nominated by
his Majesty as the three supervisors. The
first matter for their determination was,
fixing on the spot where the two penitentiary houses for the metropolis should be
erected. Various situations were proposed, and Mr. *Howard* paid due attention to all the plans, by visiting the spots,
and maturely considering all circum-
stances favourable and objectionable. The
result was, that his opinion and that of
Dr. Fothergill coincided in giving a preference

ference to Iflington, for reafons which he has ftated in his laft publication. Mr. Whately preferred the fituation of Lime-houfe. By the death-bed advice of Sir W. Blackftone, the two friends adhered to their opinion; but the matter was made an affair of obftinate contention, and remained undecided during the year 1780. At the end of it Dr. Fothergill died; upon which event, Mr. *Howard*, forefee-ing that the want of the fupport of fuch a colleague would render his future interference ufelefs, fent his refignation of the office of fupervifor in January 1781, in a letter to Earl Bathurft, which he has printed.

Now that Mr. *Howard* had freed himfelf from the engagement, which feemed to be the only obftacle between him and

that

that elegant retreat which for so many
years he had inhabited, it might naturally
be imagined that he would sit down in
repose, for the remainder of his life, satisfied with the unparalleled and successful
exertions he had made for the relief of
the most distressed portion of mankind;
and thenceforth employ himself only in
those more confined deeds of beneficence
which he had ever practised. But it was
a leading feature in his character, not to
be content with any thing short of the
greatest perfection, which every object of
his pursuit was capable of attaining; and
this principle could scarcely fail of applying itself to a subject so important as
that which had for some years occupied
his attention. Though his researches in
those foreign countries which promised

7   most

moft information, might have been fuppofed to have exhaufted that fource of
improvement, yet, on furveying fo large
à tract of Europe as yet unvifited, he
could not be fatisfied to remain unacquainted with the ufeful facts relative to
his purpofe, which might poffibly lie
there concealed. And he was convinced,
that every new vifit, even to places already
examined, would afford new inftruction.

It was therefore no furprife to thofe who
intimately knew him, to learn, that in the
fummer of 1781 he was fet out on a tour
to the capitals of Denmark, Sweden,
Ruffia, and Poland, with the further intention of revifiting Holland and part of
Germany. From this tour he returned
towards the clofe of the year. I have
before me a letter of his to a friend (the

Rev.

Rev. Mr Smith of Bedford), dated
Mofcow, September 7, 1781, whence it
appears, that thefe parts of the world were
lefs fuitable to his mode of living than
the countries through which his former
travels lay. " I thought (fays he) I
could live where any man did live; but
this northern journey, efpecially in Sweden, has pinched me:—no fruit, no garden ftuff, four bread, four milk :—but in
this city I find every luxury, even pine-
apples and *potatoes*." He mentions having declined every honour that was offered him at Peterfburgh, even that of a
foldier to attend him on his journey;
and fays, that he will not leave Mofcow
till he has made repeated vifits to the
prifons and hofpitals, fince the firft man
in the kingdom had affured him, that

his

his publication would be tranflated into Ruffian.

The year 1782 he employed in another complete furvey of the prifons in England, and another journey into Scotland and Ireland. The Irifh Houfe of Commons having appointed a gaol-committee, he reported to it the ftate of feveral of the prifons in Dublin. Other objects in that ifland alfo engaged his attention, of which an account will be given hereafter.

Spain and Portugal yet remained untouched ground. Confidering how much the fpirit of religious bigotry and civil defpotifm has thrown thefe countries back in the progrefs of modern improvement, much inftruction was not to be expected from them ; yet the very circumftance

I   of

of their difference from the reſt of Europe made their ſyſtems of police an object of curioſity. He ſailed to Liſbon in February 1783, and proceeded thence by land into Spain, paſſing from Badajos to Madrid, and through Valladolid, Burgos, and Pamplona, to France. From this laſt country he returned through Flanders and Holland to England. Travelling in Spain is a ſevere trial of patience to thoſe who have been accuſtomed to eaſy conveyance and luxurious indulgences; but, Mr. *Howard*'s wants were eaſily ſatisfied. " The Spaniards (ſays he, in a letter to the ſame friend) are very ſober, and very honeſt; and if a traveller can live ſparingly, and lie on the floor, he may paſs tolerably well through their country." From Liſbon to Madrid he could ſeldom

get

get the luxury of milk with his tea; but one morning (he tells his friend) he robbed a kid of two cups of its mother's milk. He remained, however, in perfect health and spirits; and received that mark of attention which he most of all valued, a free accefs to the prifons of all the cities he vifited, by means of letters to the magiftrates from Count Campomanes.

After a fhort repofe on his return from this tour, he made another journey in the fummer of the fame year into Scotland and Ireland, and again vifited feveral of the Englifh prifons.

His materials had now once more accumulated to fuch a mafs, as to demand communication to the public. During the laft three years his labours had been even greater than in any former

equal

equal period; yet it could not be expected, that the matter abfolutely new which he had collected fhould be proportionally great. It was, however, enough to employ him very clofely during feveral months of the year 1784, in printing an *Appendix*, and a new edition of the main work, in which all the additions were comprized. The Appendix contains all the matter of that of 1780, together with what had fince accrued. Of the latter I now proceed to give fome account.

Several new houfes of correction are defcribed under the head of *Holland*, the country which Mr. *Howard* ever found the moft fertile fource of inftruction in this branch of police. The plan of the large new workhoufe of Amfterdam muft

7   be

be well worth ftudying, as affording hints
for the conftruction of penitentiary houfes.
Germany has the addition of the prifons
of Hanover and Bremen, a minute account of the great and well regulated
workhoufe at Hamburg, and fhort notices
concerning Silefia. Of the northern
kingdoms which he now firft vifited, it
may in general be obferved, that their
models, as well with refpect to police,
as to mode of living, have been Holland and Germany; but their poverty,
and the rigour of their climate, have
made them degenerate in their imitations.
In particular, they are extremely deficient
in cleanlinefs and induftry. The new
articles, therefore, of *Denmark* and *Sweden*, though valuable for the information
they contain, yet afford little or nothing

I 3   of

of inftruction. The vaft empire of *Ruffia*, lately emerged from obfcurity to take a commanding ftation in the fyftem of Europe, and governed by uncontrouled power, at prefent directed by a fpirit of magnificent improvement, could not but offer in its inftitutions various things worthy of notice. Its police refpecting criminals, its prifons, hofpitals, and places of public education, are briefly mentioned by Mr. *Howard*; but he has found little to propofe as an example for other countries. The regulations of the great convent at Peterfburg, for the education of female children of the nobility and commoners, are given in detail, and afford fome falutary rules for the prefervation of the health of young perfons, and for promoting habits of cleanlinefs and temperance.

perance. The plan and defcription of a
magazine for medicinal herbs at Mofcow,
will be a pleafing novelty to moft readers.
Mr. *Howard* had been anticipated in his
furvey of the prifons and hofpitals of the
northern kingdoms, by that well-informed
traveller, Mr. Coxe, who publifhed a
pamphlet on the fubject in 1781, here referred to with commendation. The fhort head
of *Poland* contains little but a teftimony to
the neglected and wretched ftate of public inftitutions in that ill-governed country. All travellers have concurred in
fimilar reprefentations of the whole fyftem of affairs, internal and external, in
that unhappy feat of ariftocratical tyran-
ny; fo that it may be prefumed, there
does not exift fo determined an enemy of
innovation as not to rejoice in the change

of

of conftitution which has lately been effected there, by means of the filent and. peaceable progrefs of light and reafon.

There are various additional articles under *Flanders*, one of which relates to a great alteration for the worfe in the houfe of correction at Ghent. A once flourifhing manufactory carried on in the prifon was at an end; and the allowance of victuals to the prifoners was reduced in quantity and quality. In the account of a very offenfive prifon at Lille, Mr. *Howard* expreffes his grateful acknowledgments to Providence for his recovery from a fever caught there of the fick.

The account of *Portugal* is almoft confined to the prifons and hofpitals of Lifbon; the ftate of which, upon the whole, does credit to the government. The employ-

ment

ment of about a thoufand vagrant and
deferted children in a manufactory, is one
of the moft obfervable circumftances.

Spain, which has been long diftinguifhed for its charitable eftablifhments,
affords likewife in its criminal police
many things deferving of attention;
though the fpirit of rigour and feverity is perhaps too apparent, amidft
much laudable order and exactnefs. The
houfe of correction at Madrid, called *San
Fernando*, may vie with fome of the beft
regulated inftitutions of this nature; and
the *Hofpicio*, a kind of work-houfe, in
which extenfive manufactories are carried
on, is a good example of the union of
employment with confinement. The account of the charitable fociety of the
Hermandad del Refugio, who patrole the
ftreets

ſtreets in the evening, for the purpoſe of inviting deſtitute wanderers to a comfortable ſupper and night's lodging, will excite pleaſing ſenſations in the breaſt of every lover of humanity. The priſons of the Inquiſition, thoſe objeƈts of horror and deteſtation to every proteſtant, and now, probably, to moſt catholics, excited great curioſity in Mr. *Howard,* of which, however, all his efforts could only procure a partial gratification. Yet he has been able to communicate enough concerning thoſe of Valladolid to form a ſtriking picture of terror. On the whole, the predileƈtion he had long entertained for the Spaniſh charaƈter, was not diminiſhed by his viſit to the country; nor does he ſeem to have thought his pains in extending his enquiries to it, ill beſtowed. The

additional

additional notices in *France* chiefly relate to the Paris hofpitals. It is needlefs to dwell on thefe, fince a very accurate defcription of them has fince been given in a capital work by M. Tenon.

To the account of foreign prifons and hofpitals fucceeds a frefh furvey of the prifoners of war.

The new journies to *Scotland*, now extended as far as Invernefs, afford little but cenfure for the neglect of the prifons in that country. Under *Ireland* are introduced additional remarks on the faults and abufes ftill obfervable in the prifons there, notwithftanding a very fpirited exertion of the legiflature to amend their ftate, by framing good acts for their regulation. But, " *quid leges fine moribus*, &c." The horrid effects of that cheap poifon,

poifon, whifky, upon the health and morals of the lower claffes in that country,
are noticed by Mr. *Howard* with much
indignant difguft. A new object of attention occurred to him in the two laft
vifits to Ireland,—the *Proteftant Charter
Schools*, a noble foundation, but which he
found funk into wretched abufe notwithftanding the patronage and fuperintendance of the firft perfons in that kingdom.
Erroneous accounts of them, publifhed
by a committee, and authorized by being annexed to a printed fermon of a
prelate in their favour, were detected by
Mr. *Howard* on his vifits to fome of
them, and are expofed with his ufual
freedom.

Further accounts of the *Hulks* follow.
To the remarks on the *Gaol-fever*, Mr.
Howard

Howard adds the information, that in 1782 he did not find one perſon in this kingdom affected with that diſeaſe; but that in 1783 he had the mortification to obſerve ſeveral priſons, through original bad conſtruc- tion and neglect, relapſing to their for- mer ſtate. So eſſential is a plan of con- ſtant vigilance and inſpection, to coun- teract the lamentable tendency to abuſe in all public inſtitutions! This principle of corruption and decay in every thing human is ſo inceſſantly active, that, if not reſiſted by the timely efforts of reforma- tion, all the contrivances of wiſdom againſt natural and moral evils, would, like the dykes of Holland, perpetually ſapped and worn by the force of the elements, fall into irremediable ruin.

The remainder of this volume is taken

up

up with a review of all the English prifons, together with particulars of all the
alterations which they had undergone
fince the laft publication. The reader
will be gratified in finding, from the
number of new prifons, and new buildings and conveniences added to the old,
that the counties in general had by no
means been deficient in liberal attention
to this great object, fince it had been
brought forward and aided by Mr. *Howard*'s indefatigable exertions. At the
conclufion, among the *Tables*, is a fketch
of general heads of regulations for penitentiary houfes, which will be highly
ufeful in fuggefting a complete body of
rules and orders for fuch eftablifhments,
if ever they fhould again be thought of
in this country.

The

The printing of this copious *Appendix*, together with a complete edition of his *State of the Prisons*, into which all the additions were incorporated, making a large and closely printed quarto volume, occupied much of Mr. *Howard*'s time in the year 1784. The remainder of that, and the greater part of the next year, do not appear marked with his public services. They were, I believe, chiefly employed in domestic concerns, of which the choice of a proper place of education for his son, now rising towards manhood, was one that most interested him. But the habitude of carrying on researches into an object, which by long possession had acquired deep root in his mind, together with a new idea, collaterally allied to it, which had struck him, at length impelled

him

him once more to engage in the toils and perils of a foreign journey.

He had obferved that, notwithftanding the regulations for preferving health in prifons and hofpitals, infectious difeafes continued occafionally to arife and fpread in them : he had alfo in his travels remarked the great folicitude of feveral trading nations to preferve themfelves from that moft deftructive of all contagious diftempers, *the Plague*; and, at the fame time, he was well apprized of the rude and neglected ftate in which the police of our own country is left refpecting that object. Combining thefe ideas, he thought that a vifit to all the principal *Lazarettos*, and to countries frequently attacked by the plague, might afford much information as to the means

of

of preventing contagion in general, as well as particular inftruction concerning eftablifhments for the purpofe of guarding against peftilential infection. His intent, therefore, was nothing lefs, than to plunge into the midft of thofe dangers which by other men are fo anxiously avoided; to fearch out and confront the great foe of human life, for the fake of recognizing his features, and difcovering the moft efficacious barriers againft his affaults. Who but muft be ftruck with admiration of the firmnefs of courage, and the ardour of benevolence, which could prompt fuch a defign! As a proof of his own idea of the hazards he was to encounter, it may be mentioned, that he refolved to travel fingle and unattended; not thinking it juftifiable to

K   permit

permit any of his fervants to partake of a danger to which they were not called by motives fimilar to his own.

It was towards the end of 1785 that Mr. *Howard* fet out upon this tour, taking his way through Holland and Flanders, to the fouth of France. As, from the jealoufy and difpleafure of the French government, he was not able to obtain permiffion to vifit the eftablifhments there, or even to gain affurance of perfonal fafety, he travelled through the country as an Englifh phyfician, never took his meals in public, and entrufted his fecret only to the proteftant minifters. In a letter from Nice to the friend above-mentioned, dated January 30, 1786, he acquaints him with thefe circumftances, and fays, that he was five days at Marfeilles

feilles and four at Toulon; and, as it was thought that he could not get out of France by land, he embarked in a Genoefe veffel, and was feveral days ftriving againft wind and tide. They who at prefent conduct the government of France, I am perfuaded, will blufh at the idea, that a *Howard* was obliged to conceal his name and purpofe while carrying on in their country inquiries which had no other aim than the good of mankind!

From Nice, Mr. *Howard* went to Genoa, Leghorn, and Naples, and to the iflands of Malta and Zante. He then failed to Smyrna, and thence to Conftantinople. I have been favoured with a letter of his to Dr. Price from this metropolis, dated June 22, 1786, fome ex-

K 2   tracts

tracts from which I shall present to the reader.

" After viewing the effects of the earthquake in Sicily, I arrived at Malta, where I repeatedly visited the prisons, hospitals, poor-houses, and lazarettos, as I staid three weeks. From thence I went to Zant : as they are all Greeks, I wished to have some general idea of their hospitals and prisons, before I went into Turkey. From thence, in a foreign ship, I got a passage to Smyrna. Here I boldly visited the hospitals and prisons; but as some accidents happened, a few dying of the plague, several shrunk at me. I came thence about a fortnight ago. As I was in a miserable Turk's boat, I was lucky in a passage of six days and a half. A family arrived just before

before me, had been between two and
three months.

" I am forry to fay fome die of the
plague about us; one is juft carried before my window; yet I vifit where none
of my conductors will accompany me.
In fome hofpitals, as in the lazarettos,
and yefterday among the fick flaves, I
have a conftant headach, but in about an
hour after it always leaves me. Sir Ro-
bert Ainflie is very kind; but for the
above, and other reafons, I could not
lodge in his houfe. I am at a phyfician's, and I keep fome of my vifits a
fecret."

He defigned to proceed from Conftantinople over land to Vienna; but,
having determined, upon reflection, to
obtain by perfonal experience the fulleft

informa-

information of the mode of performing quarantine, he returned to Smyrna, where the plague then was, for the purpose of going to Venice with a *foul bill*, that would neceſſarily ſubject him to the utmoſt rigour of the proceſs. His voyage was tedious, and rendered hazardous by equinoctial ſtorms; and in the courſe of it he incurred a danger of another kind, the ſhip in which he was a paſſenger being attacked by a Tuniſian corſair, which, after a ſmart ſkirmiſh, was beaten off by the execution done by a cannon loaded with ſpike nails and bits of iron, and pointed by Mr. *Howard* himſelf. It afterwards appeared to have been the intention of the captain to blow up his veſſel, rather than ſubmit to be taken into perpetual ſlavery. It was not till the

cloſe

clofe of 1786 that Mr. *Howard* left his difagreeable quarters in the lazaretto of Venice, in which his health and fpirits fuffered confiderably. Thence he went by Triefte to Vienna. In this capital he had the honour of a private conference with the Emperor, which was conducted with the utmoft eafe and condefcenfion on the part of Jofeph II. and equal free-dom on the part of the Englifhman. A relation of this inftructive fcene in his own words, will, I doubt not, be agree-able to the reader: " The Emperor de-fired to fee me, and I had the honour of a private audience with him of above an hour and a half. He took me by the hand three times in converfation, and thanked me for the vifit. He after-wards told our Ambaffador, ' That his

K 4 country-

countryman fpoke well for prifoners; that he ufed no flowers, which others ever do, and mean nothing.' But his greateft favour to me was his immediate alterations for the relief of the prifoners*." That the late Emperor had an ardent zeal for improvement of every kind, and a ftrong defire of promoting the profperity of his fubjects, will fcarcely be denied, even by thofe who are the fevereft cenfurers of the mode in which he conducted his plans, and his extreme mutability refpecting them. He will alfo be honoured, for the readinefs with which he laid afide the etiquette of his rank, on every occafion where it obftructed him in the acquifition of knowledge, or the activity of exertion. Mr.

* Letter to Mr. Smith.

Howard

Howard returned through Germany and Holland, and arrived fafe in England early in 1787.

It was during this tour, and while he was in folitude occupying a cell of the Venice lazaretto, that he received from England two pieces of intelligence, both of which diftreffed and haraffed his mind, though the emotion they excited muft apparently have been very different. One of thefe related to the melancholy derangement of mind into which his fon had fallen, and which, after various inftances of ftrange and unaccountable behaviour, terminated at length in decided infanity. They who cannot believe that the moft benevolent of mankind could be a ftern and unnatural

parent,

parent, will fympathize in the anguifh he muft have felt on hearing (and in fuch a fituation too) of an event which blafted the deareft hopes of comfort and folace in his declining years. I, who have frequently heard him fpeak of this fon, with all the pride and affection of the kind father of an only child, cannot read without ftrong emotions, the expreffions he ufes in writing to his friend relative to this bitter calamity. When he concludes a long letter upon various topics, with the exclamation, " But, O! my fon, my fon!" I feem to perceive the efforts of a manly mind, ftriving by the aid of its internal refources to difpel a gloomy phantom, which was yet ever recurring to his imagination. But in this

emergency,

emergency, as in all others, the confo-
lations of religion were his chief re-
fuge *.

The other caufe of uneafinefs by which
his mind was agitated, will, to many, appear a very extraordinary one; fince it
arofe from a teftimony of efteem and
veneration in his countrymen, which
might be imagined to afford balm for
his wounded fpirit. During his abfence,

* To prove that Mr. *Howard* had kind and tender feelings for *domeftic* as well as for *public* occafions, will, I hope, by moft perfons be deemed a
fuperfluous tafk. For thofe who require fuch proof,
I copy the following paffage from one of his letters
to Mr. Smith. " My old fervants, John Prole,
Thomas Thomafon, and Jofeph Crockford, have had
a fad time. I hear they have been faithful, wife,
and prudent. Pleafe to thank them particularly in
my name for their conduct. Two of them, I am
perfuaded, have acted out of regard to his excellent
mother,—who, I rejoice, is *dead*."

a fcheme

a scheme had been set on foot to honour him in a manner almost unprecedented in this age and country. Without attempting to trace it to its origin, it may suffice to say, that, in a periodical work of extensive circulation, the public were called upon to testify their respect for Mr. *Howard* by a subscription, for the purpose of erecting a statue, or some other monument, to his honour. The authors of this scheme, though, doubtless, actuated by a pure and laudable admiration of illustrious virtue, yet must have been totally unacquainted with Mr. *Howard's* disposition; otherwise they would never have thought of decorating a man, whose characteristic feature had always been a solicitude to shun all notice and distinction, with one of the

most

moft glaring and prominent marks of public applaufe, which might put to the blufh modefty of a much lefs delicate texture than his. The Englifh national character (if national character can be faid to belong to fo heterogeneous a people) is by nothing fo ftrongly mark-ed, as by a coynefs and referve which fhrink from obfervation, and even to thofe who are acting for the public, render the gaze of the public eye painful. The love of glory, which is fo active a fentiment to fome of our neighbours, operates feebly upon us: many do not rife to it, and fome go beyond it. That " humble Allen," whofe difpofition it was to " do good by ftealth and blufh to find it fame," was a genuine Englifh phi-lanthropift; and fuch was Mr. *Howard*,

7   rendered,

rendered, perhaps, ſtill more averſe to
public praiſe, by a deep ſenſe of religious
humility.

A ſimilar want of acquaintance with
Mr. *Howard*'s deſigns, cauſed the pro-
poſers of this plan to attribute to him
an *extravagance* of philanthropy, which
could not but appear ridiculous to thoſe
whoſe judgment was not dazzled by the
ardour of admiration. It was aſſerted,
among real topics of applauſe, that he
was now gone abroad with the view of
extirpating the plague from Turkey;
an idea ſcarcely ſo rational, the character
of that nation conſidered, as would be
that of a miſſion to convert the Grand
Seignior to Chriſtianity. Mr. *Howard*
meant, undoubtedly, to do all the good
which ſhould lie within his compaſs in

3   that,

that, as in all other countries which he
vifited; but he was never fo romantic as
to fuppofe that he could effect that,
which would manifeftly require a total
change in the religious and political
fyftem of a great empire, of all the leaft
difpofed to change.

The project of a ftatue, however, was
eagerly adopted; the fubfcription filled,
and was adorned with the names of minifters, nobles, and perfons of diftinction;
and a committee was appointed to determine upon the beft mode of fulfilling
its purpofe. The confidential friends of
Mr. *Howard* were in a difagreeable di-
lemma; for as, on the one hand, they
could not but rejoice in the warmth of
admiration which his country teftified for
his character; fo, on the other, they well

knew

knew that its manner of difplay could not fail to give him extreme pain, and, if effected, probably banifh him for ever. On this account, they did not concur in the fcheme, and fome of them ventured publicly to throw out objections to it. Some of· its warm promoters, in reply, talked of *forcing his modefty*, and feemed determined at all events to put in execution their favourite defign. In the mean while, Mr. *Howard* was informed of this *honourable perfecution* that was preparing againft him at home; and the fenfations this intelligence occafioned in his breaft are fhewn in the following expreffions contained in a letter to the intimate friend who has already furnifhed me with various extracts. " To haften to the other very diftreffing affair: oh, why

why could not my friends, who know how
much I deteſt ſuch parade, have ſtopped
ſuch a haſty meaſure!—As a private
man, with ſome peculiarities, I wiſhed to
retire into obſcurity and ſilence.—Indeed, my friend, I cannot bear the
thought of being thus dragged out. I
immediately wrote, and hope ſomething
may be done to ſtop it. My beſt friends
muſt diſapprove it. It deranges and con-
founds all my ſchemes—my exaltation
is my fall, my misfortune *." The ſame

* He mentions in the ſame letter, as a proof how
oppoſite his wiſhes were to monumental honours,
that before he ſet out on this journey, he had given
directions, that in caſe of his death, his funeral expences ſhould not exceed ten pounds—that his tomb
ſhould be a plain ſlip of marble placed under that
of his dear Henrietta in Cardington church, with
this inſcription; *John Howard, died—aged—My hope
is in Chriſt.*

L   ſentiments

fentiments on this bufinefs are expreff-ed with equal ftrength in his letters to Dr. Price. Among other things he fays, "My trueft, intimate, and beft friends, have, I fee by the papers, been fo kind as not to fubfcribe to what you fo juftly term a *hafty meafure*. Indeed, indeed, if nothing now can be done, I fpeak *from my heart*, never poor creature was more dragged out in public."

That in all this there was no affectation, clearly appeared from the letter he fent to the fubfcribers; in which, after ex-preffing his gratitude, he difplayed fo determined a repugnance againft admit-ting of the propofed honour, deprecating it as the fevereft of punifhments, that nothing could be urged in reply, and the

bufinefs

bufinefs was dropped. Of the fum fub-
fcribed, amounting to upwards of 1500*l.*
Mr. *Howard* refufed to direct the dif-
pofal in any manner, and begged it might
no longer be termed the *Howardian fund*.
A part of it was reclaimed by the fubfcribers, but a confiderable fhare remained in a ftock; and, fince Mr. *Howard*'s
death, it has been refolved to employ it
in conferring thofe honours on his *me-*
mory which he would not accept while
living. This intention is in every refpect
ftrictly proper; and, as the noble edifice
of St. Paul's is at length deftined to re-
ceive national monuments, no commencement can be more aufpicious, than
with a name which will ever ftand fo
diftinguifhed among thofe,

Qui fui memores alios fecêre merendo.

L 2

To

To refume the narrative of Mr. *How-ard*'s public life:—After his return in 1787, he took a fhort repofe, and then went over to Ireland, and vifited moft of the county gaols and charter fchools, and came back by Scotland. In 1788 he renewed his vifit to Ireland, and completed his furvey of its gaols, hofpitals, and fchools. I fhall lay before the reader part of a letter to Dr. Price, dated from Dublin, March 23, of this year.

" My journey into this country was to make a report of the ftate of the charter fchools, which charity has been long neglected and abufed; as indeed moft public inftitutions are made private emoluments, one fheltering himfelf under the name of a bifhop, another under that of a lord; and for electioneering intereft

4.   breaking

breaking down all barriers of honour and honefty. However, Parliament now feems determined to know how its grants have been employed. I have, fince my vifits to thefe fchools in 1782, been endeavouring to excite the attention of Parliament; and fome circumftances being in my favour, a good Lord Lieutenant, a worthy Secretary (an old acquaintance), and the Firft Secretary of State, the Provoft, a fteady friend, I muft ftill purfue it; fo I next week fet out for Connaught and other remote parts of this kingdom, which indeed are more barbarous than Ruffia. By my frequent journies my ftrength is fomewhat abated, but not my courage or zeal in the caufe I am engaged in." During thefe two years, he likewife repeated his examina-

tion

tion of all the county gaols, moſt of the bridewels, and the infirmaries and hoſpitals of England, and of the hulks on the Thames, at Portſmouth and Plymouth *.

The

* It was, I believe, during his abſence in ſome of the tours of this period, that an incident happened which the reader, I hope, will think well worth re- lating. A very reſpectable-looking elderly gentleman on horſeback, with a ſervant, ſtopt at the inn neareſt Mr. *Howard*'s houſe at Cardington, and entered into converſation with the landlord concerning him. He obſerved, that characters often appeared very well at a diſtance, which could not bear cloſe inſpection; he had therefore come to Mr. *Howard*'s reſidence in order to ſatisfy himſelf concerning him. The gentleman then, accompanied by the innkeeper, went to the houſe, and looked through it, with the offices and gardens, which he found in perfect order. He next enquired into Mr. *Howard*'s character as a landlord, which was juſtly repreſented; and ſeveral neat houſes which he had built for his tenants were ſhewn him. The gentleman returned to his inn, declaring himſelf now ſatisfied with the truth of all he had heard about *Howard*. This reſpectable

ſtranger

The great variety of matter collected in these journies was methodized and put to the press in 1789. It composes a quarto volume, beautifully printed, and decorated with a number of fine plates, which, as usual, are *presented* to the public; and so eager were the purchasers of books to partake of the donation, that all the copies were almost immediately bought up. The title is, *An account of the principal Lazarettos in Europe, with various papers relative to the Plague; together with further observations on some foreign Prisons and Hospitals; with additional remarks on the present state of those in Great*

---

stranger was no other than *Lord Monboddo*; and Mr. *Howard* was much flattered with the visit, and praised his Lordship's good sense in taking such a method of coming at the truth, since he thought it worth his trouble.

Britain

Britain and Ireland. Of this work I fhall proceed to give a brief analyfis.

The firft fection relates to *Lazarettos,* beginning with that of Marfeilles, in which city the horrid ravages of the plague, within the prefent century, have left ftrong impreffions of dread of that deftroyer of mankind. Thofe of Genoa, Leghorn, Malta, Zante, Venice, and Triefte follow; the defcriptions of which are illuftrated by excellent views and plans *. Of the lazarettos of Venice a very particular account is given, comprifing the mode of reception which he

---

* In one of his letters, Mr. *Howard* mentions having met with a young Frenchman going to the academy at Rome, who for a few fequins thankfully worked under his eye, fo that he can atteft the accuracy of his draughts. Several of the plates were engraved in Holland.

himfelf

himfelf experienced, the regulations of every kind, refpecting officers and their duty, vifitation of fhips, manner of performing quarantine, and the expurgation of goods of all claffes, &c. All thefe appear to have been devifed with much judgment and prudence; but Mr. *How-ard* is obliged to give teftimony to various inftances of abufe and neglect, which greatly impair the utility of this inftitution, as well as of many others in that once celebrated and potent republic.

Sect. II. contains *propofed regulations, and a new plan for a lazaretto;* followed by obfervations on the importance of fuch an eftablifhment in England. In thefe are introduced two letters on the fubject to Mr. *Howard;* one, a long and

argumentative

argumentative one from the Englifh
merchants refiding at Smyrna; the other,
confirming their opinion, from thofe of
Salon a. Thefe commercial papers appear worthy of the moft ferious attention; and indeed it is wonderful that a
nation which boafts of good fenfe and
knowledge, fhould fo long have remained patient under a police refpecting this
matter, which anfwers no effectual purpofe of fecurity, but feems only calculated to difcourage commerce, and pro-
duce fees to perfons in office, by the moft
barefaced impofitions *.

Sect. III. confifts of *papers relative to*

---

* Such is the negligence and abfurdity refpecting
the regulations of the quarantine of *perfons*, that I
have been affured, a naval officer has been called
out of the Opera-houfe, to go on board his fhip and
perform his quarantine.

the

the plague. They commence with a set of anſwers, by different medical practitioners, to queries with which Mr. *Howard* was furniſhed by the late Dr. Jebb and myſelf. I muſt obſerve, however, that all the queries do not appear, ſome of them having been miſapprehended, or imperfectly anſwered, particularly ſuch as related to the diſcrimination of other fevers of the *typhus* genus from the plague. Theſe replies will probably be thought to add little to the ſtock of knowledge we poſſeſſed reſpecting this diſeaſe; yet it is of ſome importance, that the leading facts on which all modes of preſervation muſt be founded, *viz.* that the plague is not known to ariſe ſpontaneouſly *any where*, but is always to be traced to *contagion*; and that the diſtance

to

to which its infection extends through
the atmofphere is very fmall, are eftablifhed in them by general agreement.
The " Abftract of a curative and pre-
fervative method to be obferved in Peftilential Contagions," communicated from
the Office of Health in Venice to the
court of Ruffia; and the " Abridged Relation of the Plague of Spalato in Dal-
matia, in 1784" (both extracted from
the Italian originals by myfelf), are the
other papers in this fection. In the
latter, the medical reader will be ftruck
with the equivocal nature of the fymptoms fuppofed to difcriminate this difeafe, and the very gradual progrefs from
fufpicion to certainty as to its prefence.

Sect. IV. relates to *foreign Prifons and
Hofpitals.*

Hospitals. The employment of the gally-
flaves in the arfenal of Toulon, is the moft
obfervable circumftance relative to the
.fouth of *France.* Under *Italy* there is a
pleafing account of the improvements at
Florence, in confequence of the humane
attention of the Grand Duke (Leopold,
the prefent Emperor). This prince, befides other inftances of liberal favour to
Mr. *Howard*'s inquiries, caufed a copy of
his new code of laws to be prefented to
him, of which, on his return, Mr. *Howard* had a tranflation printed, and dif-
tributed among the heads of the law and
other perfons, in and out of parliament.
Of the Grand Duke Mr. *Howard* never
fpoke without the warmeft expreffions of
gratitude and refpect, calling him a
glorious prince, and declaring that nothing

thing could exceed his attention to whatever might promote the happiness and prosperity of his people. It is earnestly to be wished, that the same regard to the principles of justice and humanity may accompany him in the very elevated station which is now assigned him by Providence.

' *Malta*, that celebrated feat of piracy, dignified by the spirit of chivalry and devotion, affords a new and curious article. Its great hospital, which boasts of lodging the sick in a palace, and serving them in plate, is here described by one whose penetrating eye could distinguish between parade and comfort; and it undergoes some severe censure. Mr. *Howard* visited it *before* he delivered his letter of recommendation from Sir W. Hamilton

7   to

to the Grand Mafter, as well us frequently afterwards.

The *Turkifh dominions*, whence all light,
liberty, and public fpirit, are moft effectually excluded, could not be expected to yield i ftruction in police to Europe.   Yet debtors and felons are
there confined in feparate prifons, a re-
finem nt to which this country is not
yet entirely arr.ved.   The hofpitals in
the great commercial city of Smyrna
feem all to belong to the Franks, Greeks,
and Jews.   Even at Conftantinople the
Turks have few hofpitals, and thofe in
a wretched ftate.   The hofpitals for lu-
natics there, are, indeed, examples of ad-
mirable conftruction, but neglected in
their management.   Yet, amidft this dif-
regard of the human fpecies, Mr. *How-*
ard

ard found an *afylum for cats*. Such are the contradictions of man!

The inftitutions of *Vienna* fhew that fingular mixture of clemency and rigour, of care and neglect, that might be expected from the indecifive character of the fovereign. The perpetual confinement of criminals in dark, damp dungeons, as a fubftitute for capital punifhment, manifeftly appears to be as little an advantage on the fide of lenity, as it is on that of public utility. The much beaten ground of *Holland* ftill affords new obfervations, particularly refpecting the legal procefs for debt, in ufe there.

Sect. V. relates to *Scotland*; and what is new chiefly regards the charitable inftitutions of Edinburgh. As to the pri-

fons

fons there, Mr. *Howard* was obliged to remark to the Lord Provoſt, " that the ſplendid improvements carrying on in their places of entertainment, ſtreets, ſquares, bridges, &c. ſeemed to occupy all the attention of the gentlemen in office, to the total neglect of this eſſential branch of the police." This weighty animadverfion deſerves ſerious notice, as a ſtrong confirmation of thoſe charges againſt the ſpirit of luxury, which various modern philoſophers have been fond,of turning into ridicule. In fact, a ſpirit which increaſes perſonal wants and indulgences, and augments the diſtance between the higher and lower orders of ſociety, cannot but interfere with the duties, as well of charity, as of juſtice, which are owing to our fellow-creatures

of every condition. The arts of luxury
may promote knowledge, and this may
fecondarily be employed with advantage
on objects of general utility; but it is
not likely that the fame perfons whofe
minds are occupied with fchemes of
fplendor and elegant amufement, fhould
beftow attention on the coarfe and dif-
gufting offices annexed to the care of the
poor and miferable.

The fubject of *Sect*. VI. is the *Irifh
Prifons and Hofpitals*. Mr. *Howard* obferved a very liberal and humane fpirit
with refpect to prifons, prevailing among
the gentlemen of that country, difplayed
in the erection of many new gaols, the
plans of which, however, he could not
approve. The evils occafioned by the
ufe of fpirituous liquors, particularly apparent

parent in Ireland, draw from him much complaint and cenfure. It is à fhocking confideration that the intereft of the revenue fhould, in this matter, be fuffered to prevail over the good of the nation; and nothing can deferve feverer animad-verfion, than the conduct of thofe *fervants of the public*, the commiffioners of excife, who prefume to grant licences to tippling houfes in villages, contrary to the declared wifh and opinion of gentlemen who refide on the fpot, and are witneffes of their fatal confequences to the health and morals of the neighbourhood. This is indeed, reverfing the order of civil government, and elevating fubaltern interefts to ruling principles. All the hofpitals in Dublin are noticed by Mr. *Howard,* with remarks. He then

proceeds

proceeds to a furvey of all the county gaols and hofpitals in the kingdom. The county hofpitals are in fact national inftitutions, maintained in great part by the county rates and king's letter, and therefore are not fo exactly fuperintended as thofe in England, which depend upon private fubfcription for their fupport. The confequence of this is fhewn in the wretched ftate in which the greater part of them were found, the abodes of filth, hunger, neglect, and every fpecies of abufe. Yet a fpirit of improvement was beginning to operate among them, to which this free ftatement of their defects would, doubtlefs, much contribute.

Sect. VII. is devoted to an account of the *Charter-fchools* in Ireland. The public

lic detection of mifreprefentations and abufes in this great national object had excited the attention of feveral of the leading men; and Mr. *Howard* had been defired to lay his obfervations before the committee of fifteen in Dublin, who have the fuperintendance of them. He alfo made a report of their ftate before the Irifh Houfe of Commons; and, having entered heartily into the fubject, he refolved to give it a thorough inveftigation. He therefore extended his vifits to the whole of them, in number thirty-eight, and to the four provincial nurferies from which they are fupplied. The refult of his obfervations is here given, with free cenfures of defects, and candid acknowledgments of improvement. He concludes the account with fome general re-

M 3   marks

marks on the inftitution, and fome hints
for rendering it more ufeful; and, after
expreffing a wifh, that the benefits of
education were more generally extended
over Ireland than they can be by thofe
fchools, he difplays the enlarged liberality of his mind in the following fentence, which contains a maxim worthy
of being written in letters of gold. "I
hope I fhall not be thought, as a Proteftant diffenter, indifferent to the Proteftant caufe, when I exprefs my wifh, that
thefe diftinctions [between Catholic and
Proteftant] were lefs regarded in beftow-
ing the advantages of education; and that
the increafe of Proteftantifm were chiefly
trufted to the diffemination of *knowledge*
and *found morals*."

This fection is concluded, with an example

ample ftrikingly illuftrative of the eafe with which education may be extended to the whole body of poor, afforded by the truftees of the blue-coat-hofpital in Chefter, whofe report of their plan and its fuccefs is here copied: and alfo, with the rules of the Quaker's-fchool at Ackworth, excellently adapted to promote that decent and regular deportment in youth which Mr. *Howard* fo much admired. Ireland has reafon to think herfelf peculiarly indebted to him for his laborious inveftigations and free remarks on her public inftitutions. No country certainly wanted them more; and none, I believe, is better difpofed to profit by them. She has not been ungrateful to her benefactor (*that* was never her character), for in no country is the memory of Mr. *Howard* more re-

M 4   vered.

vered. During his journies there, feveral of the principal towns prefented him
with their freedom; and the Univerfity
of Dublin, with great liberality, conferred on him the honorary degree of
Doctor of Laws. Mr. *Howard*'s aver-
fion to all kinds of diftinction, and the
natural diflike of changing his ufual de-
fignation at an advanced age, prevented
him from publicly affuming this refpectable title.

Sect. VIII. relates to *Englifh Prifons
and Hofpitals*. The prifons are all fpeci-
fied in the order of the former works,
with fuch remarks as the alterations made
in them, and other circumftances, fuggefted. Many of the defcriptions of
hofpitals are new, particularly an account
of all the hofpitals for the fick in the
metropolis.

metropolis. It is probable that few inftitutions of the kind in Europe are
better conducted than thefe; yet there
are defects, both general and particular,
which Mr. *Howard* has briefly pointed
out, and which claim the attention of
thofe who are really interefted in the
utility of thefe noble charities, and do
not confider them merely as fubfervient
to private emolument. In a note under
the county gaol in Southwark, he mentions in ftrong terms of pity and indignation the ftate of fifty felons, fentenced for tranfportation in the courfe of
the preceding five years, and kept in the
moft wretched condition till an opportunity fhould offer of putting their fentence in execution. This neceffary delay of punifhment muft ever be a ftrong
objection

objection to the fcheme of diftant banifh-
ment, and gives a decided preference,
both in juftice and policy, to the plan
of penitentiary houfes, fo thoughtlefsly
abandoned for the Botany-bay fettlement.
The *injuftice*, indeed, of the interme-
diate confinement, is leffened by an act
of 24th Geo. III. which directs, that all
the time during which a convict fhall
have continued in gaol under fentence
of tranfportation, fhall be deducted out
of the term of his tranfportation. Still,
however, fuch confinement is a *different*,
and, in thefe circumftances, a *much worfe*,
punifhment, than that to which they are
fentenced.

The county bridewel at Reading occafions a note which deferves particular
attention. Mr. *Howard* has been fuppofed

3   the

the peculiar patron of *folitary confinement,* and his recommendation has caufed it to be adopted in various places, but to a degree beyond his intentions. He well knew, from manifold obfervation, that human nature could not endure, for a long time, confinement in perfect foli- tude, without finking under the burden. He had feen the moft defperate and refractory in foreign countries tamed by it; he therefore propofed in our own prifons a *temporary* treatment of this kind, as the moft effectual, yet lenient, mode of fubduing the ferocity of our criminals : but he never thought of its being made the fentence of offenders during the *whole term* of their imprifon- ment; fuch being not only extreme and fcarcely juftifiable feverity, but incon-

fiftent

fiftent with the defign of reclaiming them to habits of induftry by hard labour. He, indeed, univerfally approved of *noɛturnal folitude*, as affording an opportunity for ferious refleɛtion, and preventing thofe plans of mifchief, and mutual encouragements to villainy, which are certain to take place among criminals, when left to herd together, without infpeɛtion.

The employment of conviɛts in building a new county gaol at Oxford, with their general good behaviour in it, affords an example of the poffibility and probable good effeɛt of occupying them in ufeful labour *at home.*

The *fever wards* of the Chefter infirmary are very properly noticed, as a fpirited inftance of extending relief to

perfons

perfons fuffering under a dangerous and infectious difeafe, and, by proper regulations, rendering the contagion harmlefs to others. I am perfuaded, that the plague itfelf, thus managed, might be prevented from communicating itfelf even to thofe under the fame roof with it. Mr. *Howard* was happy to find in this city a character congenial with his own in the ardour of active benevolence, and diftinguifhed by various fuccefsful plans for the public good. To the medical reader, as well as to many others, it will be unneceffary to mention the name of Dr. *Haygarth*.

A particular account of all the *hulks* is given at the end of the Englifh gaols. The condition of thefe floating bridewels was improved in feveral refpects fince

Mr.

Mr. *Howard*'s former vifits; but, if confidered in any other light than as *temporary* places of confinement till fome better plan is adopted, they are liable to many objections, which are here ftated.

_ *Remarks on Penitentiary Houfes* follow. In thefe the writer ftates his ideas concerning their nature and object, gives the reafons which induced Dr. Fothergill and himfelf to fix on the fituation of Ifling-ton, and relates his refignation of the office of Supervifor, as formerly mentioned. The *general heads of regulations* propofed for fuch houfes in the laft Appendix, are here reprinted; and a plate is added explanatory of the plan of building he approves. It is on every account to be lamented, that Mr. *Howard* fhould not have had the fatisfaction of feeing

one

one of his favourite designs, the subject of his most laborious research and maturest reflection, carried into execution. The objection of expence was surely unworthy of a country like this, whose prosperity and resources are so magnificently displayed, when the provinces of Holland, petty states of Germany, and cantons of Switzerland, have not been afraid of incurring it. Whether the preferred scheme of *colonizing with convicts at the Antipodes*, has the advantage of it in this respect, the public are now pretty well able to determine.

In the remarks on the *gaol-fever*, repeated with a little variation from the last publication, we are informed, that since 1782, when the prisons of this kingdom were entirely free from this disease,

several

feveral fatal and alarming inftances of it had occurred. Its appearance and frequency will probably much depend upon the epidemic conftitution of the year, as long as its occafional caufes continue to fubfift; but that proper care and regulations in prifons might almoft entirely extirpate thefe caufes, there feems no reafon to doubt.

The *conclufion* expreffes the writer's fatisfaction in that humane and liberal fpirit which has fo much alleviated the diftrefs of prifoners; but laments, that here its exertions feem to ftop, and that little or nothing is done towards that moft important object, the *reformation* of offenders. From clofe obfervation he is convinced, that the *vice of drunkennefs* is the root of all the diforders of our prifons,

and

and that fome effectual means to eradicate it are neceffary, if we mean to preferve the health and amend the morals of pri-foners. Mr. *Howard* therefore fubjoins, as his final legacy towards the improve-ment of this branch of police, the *draught of a bill* for the better regulation of gaols, and the prevention of drunkennefs and rioting in them. Of this, the leading claufes are framed for the purpofe of ab-folutely prohibiting the entrance of *any liquor* into a gaol, except *milk, whey, but-termilk,* and *water,* unlefs in cafe of fick-nefs and medical prefcription. He was fully fenfible that, in this free living coun-try, the denial of even fmall beer would be deemed a fpecies of cruelty; and he doubted not that it would go far to lofe him, in the popular eftimation, the title

N   of

of the *Prisoner's Friend*: but as attaining a popularity of that kind was not his
original object, so he could bear to
forfeit it, while conscious of still pursuing
the real good of those unhappy people.
Being convinced from experience, that
there was no medium in this matter, and
that if strong liquors were at all admitted
into prisons, no bounds could be set to
their use, he thought it right to deny an
indulgence to a few, for the sake of the
essential advantage of the many. Debtors, then, while the same place of confinement serves for them and felons, must
be subjected to the same restraints. And,
to take off the objection of the hardship
this would impose upon *innocent debtors*,
it was greatly his wish, that such alterations should take place in our law for
debt,

debt, that none but *fraudulent debtors* should be liable to imprisonment, who, he justly observes, are really *criminals*. He supposes that the gentlemen of the faculty will condemn the total rejection of fermented liquors from the diet of prisoners, under the notion of their being useful as antiseptics ; and I confess I was one who pleaded with him on this subject : but he answered me with arguments which he has here stated, and they are worthy of consideration. After all, many will suppose, that in his feelings, both with respect to these privations, and to his proposed indulgences of tea, and other vegetable articles, he was in some measure under the influence of his own peculiar habits of life ; so natural is it for our judgment of particulars to be warped,

when

when our general principles remain fixed
and unaltered. The *draught of a bill*
will, I prefume, appear in moft refpects
excellent; and the great purpofe of preferving fobriety in gaols, cannot, furely,
be too much infifted on.

Mr. *Howard's* leading ideas on this
fubject were formed fome years before.
In May 1787, the Lord Chancellor, in
an excellent fpeech on a propofed. In-
folvent Bill, after difcuffing the point of
imprifonment for debt, and the nature
of fuch bills, proceeded to fome confiderations refpecting the management and
difcipline of our prifons. He faid, " he
had lately had the honour of a converfation upon the fubject, with a gentleman
who was, of all others, the beft qualified
to treat of it—he meant, Mr. *Howard,*
whofe

whose humanity, great as it was, was at least equalled by his wisdom ; for a more judicious, or a more sensible reasoner upon the topic, he never had conversed with. His own ideas had been turned to solitary imprisonment and a strict regimen, as a punishment for debt; and that notion had exactly corresponded with Mr. *Howard*'s, who had agreed with him, that the great object ought to be, when it became necessary to seclude a man from society, and imprison him for debt, to take care that he came out of prison no worse a man in point of health and morals than he went in." His Lordship afterwards recited a story which Mr. *Howard* had told him, in proof of the corruption and licentiousness of our prisons. A Quaker, he said, called upon

him

him to go with him and witneſs a ſcene
which, if he were to go ſingly, would,
he feared, be too much for his feelings:
it was, to viſit a friend in diſtreſs—a
perſon who had lately gone into the
King's-bench priſon. When they arrived, they found the man half-drunk,
playing at fives. Though greatly ſhocked
at the circumſtance, they aſked him to
go with them to the coffee-room, and take
a glaſs of wine. He refuſed, ſaying he
had drank ſo much punch, that he could
not drink wine—however, he would call
in upon them before they went away.
Mr. *Howard* and his friend returned, with
feelings very different from thoſe with
which they entered the place, but not leſs
painful.

The volume concludes with ſeveral
curious

curious and valuable *tables*, which will probably be uſed for reference at future diſtant periods. The enumeration of all the priſoners in England at his viſits in 1787 and 1788, ſhews an alarming increaſe, though in ſome meaſure to be accounted for, from a long ſuſpenſion of the uſual tranſportation. They amount to 7482.

Mr. *Howard* remained but a ſhort time at home after the printing of this work. In the concluſion of it he had declared his intention "again to quit his native country, for the purpoſe of reviſiting Ruſſia, Turkey, and ſome other countries, and extending his tour in the eaſt." The reaſon he has aſſigned for this determination, is, "a ſerious deliberate conviction that he was purſuing the path of his duty;" and it cannot be doubted, that this confideration was now, as it ever had been, his leading principle of action. But if it be afked, what was his more peculiar object in this new journey, no decifive anfwer, I believe, can be given by thofe who enjoyed the moft of his confidence. I had various converfations with him on the fubject; and I found rather a wifh to have objects of enquiry pointed out to him by others, than any fpecific views prefent to his own mind. As, indeed, his pur-pofe was to explore regions entirely new to him, and of which the police refpect-ing his former objects was very imper-fectly known to Europe (for the Turkifh dominions in Afia, Egypt, and the Bar-bary coaft, were in his plan of travels),

he

he could not doubt that important fubjects for obfervation would offer themfelves unfought. With refpect to that
part of his tour in which he was to go
over ground he had already trodden, I
conceive that he expected to do good in
that *cenforial character*, which his repeated
publications, known and attended to all
over Europe, gave him a right to affume;
and which he had before exercifed to the
great relief of the miferable in various
countries. If to thefe motives be added
the long formed habitude of purfuing a
certain track of enquiry, and an inquie-
tude of mind proceeding from domeftic
misfortune, no caufe will be left to wonder at fo fpeedy a renewal of his toils
and dangers.

He had refolved to go this journey too,

without

without an attendant; and it was not till after the moſt urgent and affectionate entreaties, that his ſervant obtained permiſſion to accompany him. Before he ſet out, he and his very intimate and highly reſpected friend, Dr. Price, took a moſt affectionate and pathetic leave of each other. From the age and infirmities of the one, and the hazards the other was going to encounter, it was the foreboding of each of them that they ſhould never meet again in this world; and their farewell correſponded with the ſolemnity of ſuch an occaſion. The reader's mind will pauſe upon the parting embrace of two ſuch men; and revere the mixture of cordial affection, tender regret, philoſophic firmneſs, and chriſtian reſignation,

.tion, which their minds muſt have diſ‑
played.

It was in the beginning of July 1789 that he arrived in Holland. Thence he proceeded through the north of Germany, Pruſſia, Courland, and Livonia, to St. Peterſburgh. From this capital he went to Moſcow. Some extracts of a letter to Dr. Price dated from this city, September 22, 1789, will, I doubt not, be accept‑able, as one of the lateſt records of his career of benevolence.

" When I left England, I firſt ſtopped at Amſterdam, and proceeded to Oſna‑burgh, Hanover, Brunſwick, and Berlin; then to Konigſberg, Riga, and Peterſ‑burgh; at all which places I viſited the priſons and hoſpitals, which were all flung open to me, and in ſome, the bur‑

gomaſters

gomaſters accompanied me into the dungeons, as well as into the other rooms of
confinement. I arrived a few days ago
in this city, and have begun my rounds.
The hoſpitals are in a ſad ſtate. Upwards
of ſeventy thouſand ſailors and recruits
died in them laſt year. I labour to con-
vey the torch of philanthropy into theſe
diſtant regions.——I am quite well—the
weather clear—the mornings freſh—thermometer 48, but fires not yet begun.
I wiſh for a mild winter, and then ſhall
make ſome progreſs in my European ex-
pedition. My medical acquaintance give
me but little hope of eſcaping the plague
in Turkey. I do not look back, but
would readily endure any hardſhips, and
encounter any dangers, to be an honour
to my Chriſtian profeſſion."

From

From Mofcow he took his course to the very extremity of European Ruffia, extended as it now is to the fhores of the Black-fea, where long dreary tracts of defert are terminated by fome of thofe new eftablifhments, which have coft fuch immenfe profufion of blood and treafure to two vaft empires, now become neigh-bours and perpetual foes. Here, at the diftance of 1,500 miles from his native land, he fell a victim to difeafe, the ravages of which, among unpitied multitudes, he was exerting every effort to reftrain. *Finis vitæ nobis luctuofus, amicis trifis, extraneis etiam ignotifque non fine cura!*

From the faithful and intelligent fervant who accompanied him (Mr. Thomas Thomafon), I have been favoured with

with an account of various particulars relative to his laft illnefs, which I fhall
give to the reader in the form in which
I received it.

" The winter being far advanced on
the taking of Bender, the commander of
the Ruffian army at that place gave permiffion to many of the officers to vifit
their friends at Cherfon, as the feverity of
the feafon would not admit of a continuance of hoftilities againft the Turks.
Cherfon, in confequence, became much
crowded; and the inhabitants teftified their
joy for the fuccefs of the Ruffians by
balls and mafquerades. Several of the
officers, of the inhabitants of Cherfon, and
of the gentry in the neighbourhood, who
attended thefe balls, were almoft immediately afterwards attacked with fevers;
and

and it was Mr. *Howard*'s idea, that the infection had been brought by the officers from Bender. Amongſt the number who caught this contagion was a young lady who reſided about ſixteen miles from Cherſon. When ſhe had been ill ſome little time, Mr. *Howard* was earneſtly requeſted to viſit her. He ſaw her firſt on Sunday, December 27. He viſited her again in the middle of the week, and a third time on the Sunday following, January 3. On that day he found her ſweating very profuſely; and, being unwilling to check this by uncovering her arm, he paſſed his under the bed-clothes to feel her pulſe. While he was doing this, the effluvia from her body were very offenſive to him, and it was always his own opinion that he then caught the fever.

4   She

She died on the following day. Mr. *How-ard* was much affected by her death, as he had flattered himfelf with hopes of her amendment. From January 3d to the 8th he fcarcely went out*; but on that day he went to dine with Admiral Mont-gwinoff, who lived about a mile and a half from his lodgings. He ftaid later than ufual; and when he returned, found himfelf unwell, and thought he had fome-thing of the gout flying about him. He immediately took fome Sal Volatile in a little tea, and thought himfelf better till three or four on Saturday morning, when feeling not fo well, he repeated the Sal Volatile. He got up in the morning,

---

* There feems fome miftake here, as there is a full report in his memorandums, of a vifit to the hofpitals in Cherfon, dated January 6.

and

and walked out; but, finding himself worse, soon returned and took an emetic. On the following night he had a violent attack of fever, when he had recourse to his favourite remedy, James's powder, which he regularly took every two or four hours till Sunday the 17th. For though Prince Potemkin sent his own phyfician to him, immediately on being acquainted with his illness, yet his own prefcriptions were never interfered with during this time. On the 12th he had a kind of fit, in which he suddenly fell down, his face became black, his breathing difficult, and he remained infenfible for half an hour. On the 17th he had another fimilar fit. On the 18th he was feized with hiccuping, which continued on the next day, when he took fome mufk

O   draughts

draughts by direction of the phyfician. About feven o'clock on Wednefday morning, the 20th of January, he had another fit, and died in about an hour after. He was perfectly fenfible during his illnefs, except in the fits, till within a very few hours of his death. This event he all along expected to take place; and he often faid, that he had no other wifh for life than as it gave him the means of relieving his fellow-creatures.

During his illnefs he received a letter from a friend, who mentioned having lately feen his fon at Leicefter, and expreffed his hopes that Mr. *Howard* would find him better on his return to England. When this account was read to him, it affected him much. His expreffions of pleafure were particularly ftrong, and he often

often defired his fervant, if ever by the bleffing of God, his fon was reftored, to tell him how much he prayed for his happinefs. He made a will* on the Thurfday before he died; and was buried, at his own requeft, at the villa of M. Dauphiné, about eight miles from Cherfon, where a monument is erected over his grave. He made the obfervation, that he fhould here be at the fame diftance from heaven, as if brought back to England. While in Cherfon, he faw the accounts of the demolition of the Baftille, which feemed to afford him a very particular pleafure; and he thought it pof-fible, the account he had himfelf pub-

---

* This muft probably have been only fome directions to his executors, as his will is dated in 1787.

lifhed

lifhed of it, might have contributed to this event."

On this relation, the general exactnefs of which may, I doubt not, be fully relied on, I fhall only make a medical remark or two. Notwithftanding Mr. *Howard*'s conviction of having caught the contagion from the young lady, I think the diftance of time between his laft vifit to her and his own feizure, makes the fact dubious. Contagion thus fenfibly received, ufually, I believe, operates in a lefs period than five days *. Perhaps his vifit to the hofpitals on the 6th, or his late return from the Admiral's on the 8th, in a cold feafon and

* According to Dr. *Lind,* its effects, fhivering and ficknefs, are inftantaneous. See *Differt. on Fevers and Infection. Chap.* ii. *fect.* I.

unwholefome

unwholefome climate, will better account for it. The nature of his complaint is not very clear, for it is very uncommon for the fenfes to remain entire till the laft, in a fever of the low or putrid kind; nor are fits, refembling epileptic attacks, among the ufual fymptoms of fuch a difeafe. That a wandering gout might make part of his indifpofition, is not very improbable, as it was a diforder to which he was conftitutionally liable, though his mode of living prevented any fevere paroxyfms of it. At any rate, his difeafe was certainly attended with debility of the vital powers, and therefore the long and frequent ufe of James's powders muft have been prejudicial. And I think it highly probable, that Mr. *Howard*'s name may be added to the numerous lift of

thofe,

thofe, whofe lives have been facrificed to
the empirical ufe of a medicine of great
activity, and therefore capable of doing
much harm as well as good.

It was Mr. *Howard*'s written requeft,
that his papers fhould be corrected and
fitted for publication by Dr. Price and
myfelf. The declining ftate of health
of Dr. Price*, has caufed the bufinefs to
devolve

* Whilft I am engaged in this work, Dr. PRICE
has followed his friend to the grave. A character
fo illuftrious will, doubtlefs, have all juftice done it
by fome pen qualified to difplay its various merits.
May I be permitted, however, to take this occafion
of mingling my regrets with thofe of his other
friends and admirers, and offering a fmall tribute to
the memory of one of the moft excellent of men!
Though during life the advanced ftation he occupied in political controverfy rendered his name
as obnoxious to fome, as it was cherifhed and re-
vered by others, yet now he is gone to that place
where

deyolve folely on me, and I have executed it to the beft of my power. Little was requifite to be done to the greateft part, which he had himfelf copied out fair. The reft was with fome difficulty to be compiled out of detached and broken memorandums; but in thefe his own words are as much as poffible preferved.

where all worldly differences are at an end, it may be hoped, that the liberal of all denominations will concur, in refpecting a long courfe of years fpent in the unremitted application of eminent abilities and acquirements, to the promotion of what he regarded as the greateft good of his fellow-creatures. A character in which were combined fimplicity of heart, with depth of underftanding,—ardent love of truth, with true Chriftian charity and humility;—high zeal for the public interefts, with perfect freedom from all private views; cannot be ultimately injured by the petulance of wit, or the invectives of eloquence. Dr. Price's reputation as a moralift, philofopher, and politician, may fafely be committed to impartial pofterity.

O 4   Of

Of this Supplement I fhall give a general account, as I have done of the former parts of his works.

The order and regularity of *Holland* ftill afford ufeful defcriptions, and fome of the abufes which even there had crept in, feem to have been corrected fince Mr. *Howard*'s vifits. The friend to humanity has yet, however, to lament the continued ufe of the torture there, to force confeffion. The ftate of the prifons in *Ofnaburgh*, *Hanover*, and *Brunfwick*, is again dwelt upon with fome minutenefs, obvioufly becaufe the writer thought there was fome probability of his attracting, in a more peculiar manner, the notice of thofe who have the power of remedying their defects. Who will not fympathize with him in the difappointment

he

he expreſſes in this inſtance, and bewail the ſtrange fatality by which the utmoſt barbarity of the torture is retained in the dominions of a mild and enlightened Sovereign, whoſe interpoſition could not but be efficacious in ſuppreſſing it!

At *Berlin* and *Spandau* the inſtitutions appear to preſerve the good order in which they were left by the Great Frederic. *Konigſberg* ſeems to ſhew the neglect incident to places diſtant from the ſeat of government. In a note under this place, Mr. *Howard* makes an acknowledgment of the attention with which his remarks have been honoured in various foreign countries, and properly adduces it as a reaſon for his adoption of that cenſorial manner of noting abuſes, which,

which, in his later journies, he has not scrupled freely to employ.

At St. *Peterſburgh* he had the pleaſure to obſerve ſeveral improvements in the hoſpitals, probably in great part owing to his own ſuggeſtions. Under *Cronſtadt* he finds occaſion, however, to animadvert upon an alteration in the plan of diet, generally adopted throughout the marine and military hoſpitals of Ruſſia, which, in his opinion, is highly prejudicial. This alteration conſiſts in changing milk, and various other articles, conſtituting the uſual liquid and middle diet of the ſick, for the ſtronger and leſs digeſtible food of men in health. The priſons at *Moſcow* ſeem greatly neglected by thoſe whoſe office it is to ſuperintend them; but the charity diſplayed by individuals

dividuals towards the poor wretches confined in them, gave Mr. *Howard* a favourable idea of the humane difpofition
of the nation, confirmed by what he faw
of their manners in his travels.

He now haftened to thofe, fcenes, where
a deftructive war, co-operating with an
unwholefome climate, produced fuch
evils, aggravated by neglect and inhu-
manity, that they gave him no other occupation than to lament and complain.
After all the allowances that candour demands, for inevitable wants and hardfhips
in the diftant pofts of a newly poffeffed
country, and during the heighth of widely
extended military operations, the Ruffian commanders cannot be vindicated
from an inattention to the lives and comforts of their foldiers, greater, as Mr.
Howard

Howard obferves, than he had feen in any other country. Ignorance, abufe, mifmanagement, and deficiency, feem at their very fummit in the military hofpitals of *Cherfon, Witowka,* and *St. Nicholas.* The lively pictures he has drawn of the diftreffes he here witneffed, and his pathetic defcription of the fufferings of the poor recruits, marched from their diftant homes to thefe melancholy regions, muft awaken in every feeling breaft a warm indignation againft the fchemes of ambitious defpotifm, however varnifhed over with the colouring of glory, or even of national utility. No leffon ought to be more forcibly impreffed on mankind, than, that uncontrouled power in one or few, notwithftanding it may occafionally be exercifed in fplendid and even beneficent

cent defigns, is on the whole abfolutely inconfiftent with the happinefs of a people *. The Emprefs of Ruffia's unjuft feizure of Leffer and Crim Tartary, has been the caufe of miferies not to be calculated, to her own fubjects and thofe of Turkey, and has endangered the tranquillity of all Europe.

I fhall conclude this review of the works and public fervices of Mr. *Howard* with brief annals of his more than Herculean labours, during the laft feventeen years of his life.

1773. High-fheriff of Bedfordfhire. Vifited many county and town gaols.

---

* Scilicet ut Turno contingat regia conjunx,
Nos, animæ viles, inhumata infletaque turba,
Sternamur campis.   · *Æn*. xi.

1774. Completed his furvey of Englifh gaols. Stood candidate to repreprefent the town of Bedford.

1775. Travelled to Scotland, Ireland, France, Holland, Flanders, and Germany.

1776. Repeated his vifit to the above countries, and to Switzerland. During thefe two years revifited all the Englifh gaols.

1777. Printed his ftate of prifons.

1778. Travelled through Holland, Flanders, Germany, Italy, Switzerland, and part of France.

1779. Revifited all the counties of England and Wales, and travelled into Scotland and Ireland. Acted as Supervifor of the Penitentiary Houfes.

1780.

1780. Printed his firft Appendix.

1781. Travelled into Denmark, Sweden, Ruffia, Poland, Germany, and Holland.

1782. Again furveyed all the Englifh prifons, and went into Scotland and Ireland.

1783. Vifited Portugal, Spain, France, Flanders, and Holland: alfo, Scotland and Ireland; and viewed feveral Englifh prifons.

1784. Printed the fecond Appendix, and a new edition of the whole works.

1785.
1786.
1787.
From the clofe of the firft of thefe years, to the beginning of the laft, on his tour through Holland, France, Italy, Malta, Turkey, and Germany. Afterwards, went to Scotland and Ireland.

1788.

1788. Revifited Ireland; and during this
and the former year, travelled
over all England.

1789. Printed his work on Lazarettos,
&c. Travelled through Holland,
Germany, Pruffia, and Livonia,
to Ruffia and Leffer Tartary.

1790. January 20. Died at Cherfon.

Having thus traced the footfteps of
this great philanthropift from the cradle
to the grave, and followed them with
clofe infpection in that part of his courfe
which comprehends his more public life,
it only remains, to affemble thofe features
of character which have been difplayed in
his actions, and to form them, in conjunction with fuch minuter ftrokes as ftu-
dious obfervation may have enabled me

to

to draw, into a faithful portraiture of the *man.*

The firſt thing that ſtruck an obſerver on acquaintance with Mr. *Howard,* was a ſtamp of extraordinary vigour and energy on all his movements and ex-preſſions. An eye lively and penetrating, ſtrong and prominent features, quick gait, and animated geſtures, gave promiſe of ardour in forming, and vivacity in exe-cuting his deſigns*. At no time of his life,

---

* Mr. *Howard,* though frequently requeſted, would never ſit for his picture; it is therefore no wonder that the portraits of him, given in various works, ſhould be all totally unlike. The moſt reſembling likeneſs, by much, is a head ſketched by an artiſt in London, engraved in Dublin, and copied for this work. It is ſomewhat of a caricature, but has very exactly the expreſſion of his counte-nance when in a very ſerious attentive mood. After his death, Prince Potemkin had two plaſter caſts

taken

life, I believe, was he without fome object of warm purfuit; and in every thing
he purfued, he was indefatigable in aim-
ing at perfection. Give him a hint of
any thing he had left fhort, or any new
acquifition to be made, and while you
might fuppofe he was deliberating about
it, you were furprifed with finding *it
was done*. Not Cæfar himfelf could
better exemplify the poet's

Nil actum credens, dum quid fupereffet agendum.

I remember that, having accidentally
remarked to him that amongft the London prifons he had omitted *the Tower*, he
was fo ftruck with the deficiency (though

taken from his face, one for himfelf, the other for
the fervant of Mr. *Howard*.

of

öf trifling confequence, fince confinement there is fo rare), that at his very firft leifure he ran to London, and fupplied it. Nor was it only during a fhort period of ardour that his exertions were thus awakened. He had the ftill rarer quality of being able, for any length of time; to bend all the powers and faculties of his mind to one point, unfeduced by every allurement which curiofity or any other affection might throw in his way, and unfufceptible of that fatiety and difguft which are fo apt to fteal upon a protracted purfuit. Though by his early travels he had fhewn himfelf not indifferent to thofe objects of tafte and information which ftrike the cultivated mind in a foreign country, yet in the tours exprefsly made for the purpofe of examining

prifons

prifons and hofpitals, he appears to have had eyes and ears for nothing elfe; at leaft he fuffered no other object to detain him or draw him afide *. Impreffed with the idea of the importance of his defigns, and the uncertainty of human life, he was impatient to get as much done as poffible within the allotted limits. And in this difpofition confifted that *enthufiafm* by which the public fuppofed him actuated; for otherwife, his cool and fteady temper gave no idea of the character ufually diftinguifhed by that appellation. He followed his plans, indeed, with wonderful vigour and con-

* He mentioned being once prevailed upon in Italy, to go and hear fome extraordinarily fine mufic; but, finding his thoughts too much occupied by it, he would never repeat the indulgence.

ftancy,

fancy, but by no means with that heat
and eagernefs, that inflamed and exalted
imagination, which denote the enthufiaft.
Hence, he was not liable to catch at partial reprefentations, to view facts through
fallacious mediums, and to fall into thofe
miftakes which are fo frequent in the
refearches of the man of fancy and warm
feeling. Some perfons, who only knew
him by his extraordinary actions, were
ready enough to beftow upon him that
fneer of contempt, which men of cold
hearts and felfifh difpofitions are fo apt
to apply to whatever has the fhew
of high fenfibility. While others, who
had a flight acquaintance with him,
and faw occafional features of phlegm,
and perhaps harfhnefs, were difpofed to
queftion his feeling altogether, and to

P 3 attribute

attribute his exertions either merely to a
fenfe of duty, or to habit and humour.
But both thefe were erroneous conclu-
fions. He felt as a man fhould feel; but
not fo as to miflead him, either in the
eftimate he formed of objects of utility,
or in his reafonings concerning the means
by which they were to be brought into
effect. The reformation of abufes, and
the relief of mifery, were the two great
purpofes which he kept in view in all
his undertakings; and I have equally
feen the tear of fenfibility ftart into his
eyes on recalling fome of the diftrefsful
fcenes to which he had been witnefs, and
the fpirit of indignation flafh from them
on relating inftances of bafenefs and op-
preffion. Still, however, his conftancy
of mind and felf-collection never deferted
him.

him. He was never agitated, never off his guard; and the unfpeakable advantages of fuch a temper in the fcenes in which he was engaged, need not be dwelt upon.

His whole courfe of action was fuch a trial of intrepidity and fortitude, that it may feem altogether fuperfluous to fpeak of his poffeffion of thefe qualities. He had them, indeed, both from nature and principle. His nerves were firm; and his conviction of marching in the path of duty made him fearlefs of confequences. Nor was it only on great occafions that this ftrength of mind was fhown. It raifed him above falfe fhame, and that awe which makes a coward of many a brave man in the prefence of a fuperior. No one ever lefs " feared the face

P 4   of

of man," than he. No one hefitated lefs in fpeaking bold truths, or avowing obnoxious opinions. His courage was equally paffive and active. He was prepared to make every facrifice that a regard to ftrict veracity, or rigorous duty, could enjoin; and it cannot be doubted, that, had he lived in an age when afferting his civil and religious rights would have fubjected him to martyrdom, not a more willing martyr would ever have afcended the fcaffold, or embraced the ftake.

The refolute temper of Mr. *Howard* difplayed itfelf in a certain peremptorinefs, which, when he had once determined, rendered him unyielding to perfuafion or diffuafion, and urged him on to the accomplifhment of his purpofe, regardlefs of obftacles. He expected prompt

obedience

obedience in thofe from whom he had a right to require it, and was not a man to be treated with negligence and inatten-tion. He was, however, extremely con-fiderate, and fufficiently indulgent to human frailties; and a good-will to pleafe him could fcarcely fail of its effect. That his commands were reafonable, and his expectations moderate, may be infer-red from the long continuance of moft of his fervants with him, and his fteady at-tachment to many of thofe whom he employed. His means of enforcing com-pliance were chiefly rewards; and the withholding them was his method of fhowing difpleafure*.

The

* The following characteriftic anecdote was com-municated to me by a gentleman who travelled in a chaife

The ſpirit of independence by which he was ever diſtinguiſhed, had in him the only foundation to be relied on, *moderate deſires.*

chaiſe with him from Lancaſhire to London in 1777. Mr. *Howard* obſerved, that he had found few things more difficult to manage than poſt-chaiſe drivers, who would ſeldom comply with his wiſhes of going ſſow or faſt, till he adopted the following method. At the end of a ſtage, when the driver had been perverſe, he deſired the landlord to ſend for ſome poor induſtrious widow, or other proper object of charity, and to introduce ſuch perſon and the driver together. He then paid the latter his fare, and told him, that as he had not thought proper to attend to his repeated requeſts as to the manner of being driven, he ſhould not make him any preſent; but, to ſhow him that he did not withhold it out of a principle of parſimony, he would give the poor perſon preſent double the ſum uſually given to a poſtillion. This he did, and diſmiſſed the parties. He had not long practiſed this mode, he ſaid, before he experienced the good effects of it on all the roads where he was known.

A more extraordinary inſtance of his determined ſpirit

defires: Perfectly contented with the competence which Providence had beſtowed on him, he never had a thought of increaſing it; and, even when in a ſituation to expect a family, he made it a

ſpirit has been related to me. Travelling once in the king of Pruſſia's dominions, he came to a very narrow piece of road, admitting only one carriage, where it was enjoined on all poſtillions entering at each end, to blow their horns by way of notice. His did ſo; but, after proceeding a good way, they met a courier travelling on the king's buſineſs, who had neglected this precaution. The courier ordered Mr. *Howard*'s poſtillion to turn back; but Mr. *Howard* remonſtrated, that he had complied with the rule, while the other had violated it; and therefore that he ſhould inſiſt on going forwards. The courier, relying on an authority, to which, in that country, every thing muſt give way, made uſe of high words, but in vain. As neither was diſpoſed to yield, they ſat ſtill a long time in their reſpective carriages: at length the courier gave up the point to the ſturdy Engliſhman, who would on no account *renounce his rights.*

rule

rule with himfelf to lay up no part of his annual income, but to expend in fome ufeful or benevolent fcheme the fuperfluity of the year. Left this fhould be converted into a charge of careleffnefs in providing for his own, it may be pro-per to mention, that he had the beft-grounded expectations, that any children he might have, would largely partake of the wealth of their relations. Thus he preferved his heart from that contami-nation, which (taking in the whole of life) is perhaps the difeafe moft fre-quently attendant on a ftate of profperity, —*the luft of growing rich*; a paffion, which is too often found to fwallow up liberality, public fpirit, and, at laft, that independency, which it is the beft ufe of wealth to fecure. By this temper of mind

mind he was elevated to an immeafur-
able diftance above every thing mean and
fordid; and in all his tranfactions he difplayed a fpirit of honour and generofity,
that might become the " blood of the
Howards" when flowing in its nobleft
channels.

Had Mr. *Howard* been lefs provided
with the goods of fortune, his independency would have found a refource in *the
fewnefs of his wants*; and it was an ineftimable advantage which he brought to
his great work, an advantage perhaps
more uncommon in this country than
any of thofe already mentioned, that he
poffeffed a command over all corporeal
appetites and habitudes, not lefs perfect
than that of any ancient philofopher, or
modern afcetic. The ftrict regimen of

7.   diet

diet which he had adopted early in life from motives of health, he afterwards perfevered in through choice, and even extended its rigour, fo as to reject all thofe indulgences which even the moft temperate confider as neceffary for the prefervation of their ftrength and vigour. Animal foods, and fermented and fpirituous drinks, he utterly difcarded from his diet. Water and the plaineft vegetables fufficed him. Milk, tea, butter, and fruit, were his luxuries; and he was equally fparing in the quantity of food, and indifferent as to the ftated times of taking it. Thus he found his wants fupplied in almoft every place where *man* exifted, and was as well provided in the pofadas of Spain and caravanferas of Turkey, as in the inns and hotels

3   of

of England and France. Water was one of his principal neceffaries, for he was a very Muffulman in his ablutions; and if nicety or delicacy had place with him in any refpect, it was in the perfect cleanlinefs of his whole perfon. He was equally tolerant of heat, cold, and all the viciffitudes of climate; and, what is more wonderful, not even fleep feemed neceffary to him, at leaft at thofe returns and in thofe proportions in which mankind in general expect it. How well he was capable of enduring fatigue, the amazing journies he took by all modes of conveyance, without any intervals of what might be called repofe (fince his only baiting places were his proper fcenes of action), abundantly teftify. In fhort, no human body was probably ever more perfectly

the

the fervant of the mind by which it was
actuated; and all the efforts of the ftrong-
eft conftitution, not inured to habits of
felf-denial, and moral as well as corporeal exercife, would have been unequal
to his exertions *.

With·

* The following account of his mode of travelling, communicated to me by a gentleman in Dublin, who had much free converfation with him, and
the fubftance of which I well recollect to have heard
from himfelf, will, I doubt not, prove interefting.
" When he travelled in England or Ireland, it was
generally on horfeback, and he rode about forty
Englifh miles a day. He was never at a lofs for
an inn. When in Ireland, or the Highlands of Scotland, he ufed to ftop at one of the poor cabins that
ftick up a rag by way of fign, and get a little milk.
When he came to the town he was to fleep at, he
befpoke a fupper, with wine and beer, like another traveller, but made his man attend him, and
take it away, whilft he was preparing his bread and
milk. He always paid the waiters, poftillions, &c.
liberally, becaufe he would have no difcontent or
difpute,

With refpect to the character of his underftanding, that, too, was as happily adapted to the great bufinefs in which he engaged. He had not, in a high degree, that extenfive comprehenfion, that faculty of generalizing, which is faid to

difpute, nor fuffer his fpirits to be agitated for fuch a matter; faying, that in a journey that might coft three or four hundred pounds, fifteen or twenty pounds addition was not worth thinking about. When he travelled on the continent, he ufually went poft in his own chaife, which was a German one that he bought for the purpofe. He never ftopped till he came to the town he meant to vifit, but travelled all night, if neceffary; and from habit could fleep very well in the chaife for feveral nights together. In the laft tour but one he travelled twenty days and nights together without going to bed, and found no inconvenience from it. He ufed to carry with him a fmall tea-kettle, fome cups, a little pot of fweetmeats, and a few loaves. At the poft-houfe he could get his water boiled, fend out for milk, and make his repaft, while his man went to the *auberge.*"

Q   diftinguifh

distinguish the man of genius, but which, without a previous collection of authentic materials, is ever apt to lead into erroneous speculations. He was rather a man of detail; of laborious accuracy and minute examination; and therefore he had the proper qualities for one who was to lead the way in researches where all was ignorance, confusion, and local custom. Who but such a man could have collected a body of information, which has made even professional men acquainted with interesting facts that they never before knew; and has given the English reader a more exact knowledge of practices followed in Russia and Spain, than he before had of those in his own country? This minuteness of detail was what he ever regarded as his peculiar province.

As

As he was of all men the moſt modeſt eſtimator of his own abilities, he was uſed to ſay, " I am the *plodder*, who goes about to collect materials for men of genius to make uſe of." Let thoſe who look with faſtidiouſneſs upon long tables of rules and orders, and meaſurements of cells and work-rooms, given in feet and inches, conſider, that when a ſcheme is brought into practice, theſe ſmall cir-cumſtances *muſt* have their place; and that the moſt ingenious plans often fail in their execution for want of adjuſt-ment in the nicer parts. Perhaps even the great Frederic of Pruſſia was more indebted for ſucceſs to the exactneſs of his diſpoſitions in every minute particu-lar connected with practice, than to deep and ſublime views of general principles.

Q 2   From

From a fimilar caft of mind, Mr.
Howard was a friend to fubordination,
and all the decorums of regular fociety;
nor did he diflike vigorous exertions of
civil authority, when directed to laudable
purpofes. He interfered little in dif-
putes relative to the theory of government; but was contented to take fyftems
of fovereignty as he found them eftablifhed in various parts of the world,
fatisfied with prompting fuch an application of their powers as might promote
the welfare of the refpective communities. A ftate of imprifonment being
that in which the rights of men are, in
great part, at leaft, fufpended, it was natural that his thoughts fhould be more
converfant with a people as the fubjects,
than as the fource, of authority. Yet

he

he well knew, and properly valued, the ineftimable bleffings of political freedom, as oppofed to defpotifm; and, among the nations of Europe, he confidered the Dutch and Swifs as affording the beft examples of a ftrict and fteady police, conducted upon principles of equity and humanity. To the character of the Dutch he was, indeed, peculiarly partial; and frequently afferted, that he fhould prefer Holland for his place of refidence, to any other foreign country. I can add, from undoubted authority, that Mr. *Howard* was one of thofe who (in the language of the great Lord Chatham) " rejoiced that America had refifted," and triumphed in her final fuccefs; that he was principally attached to the popular part of our conftitution;

Q 3   and

and that in his own county he diftinguifhed himfelf by a fpirited oppofition
to ariftocratical influence.

His peculiar habits of life, and the ex-
clufive attention he beftowed in his later
years on a few objects, caufed him to
appear more averfe to fociety than I
think he really was;. and it. has been
mentioned as an unfortunate circumftance, that his fhynefs and referve frequently kept him out of the way of perfons 'from whom he might have derived much ufeful information. But it
is vain to defire things incompatible.
Mr. *Howard* can fcarcely be denied to
have chofen the beft way, upon the whole,
of conducting his enquiries; and if he
had been a more *companionable* man, more
ready to indulge his own curiofity, and

gratify

gratify that of others, he would no longer
have poffeffed one of the chief advantages he brought to his great work.
Yet while he affiduoufly fhunned all en-
gagements which would have involved
him in the forms and diffipation of fociety, he was by no means difinclined to
enter into converfations on his particular topics; on the contrary, he was often
extremely communicative, and would
enliven a fmall circle with the moft
entertaining relations of his travels and
adventures.

Mr. *Howard* had in a high degree
that refpectful attention to the *female
fex* which fo much characterifes the *gentleman*. Perhaps, indeed, I may here
be referring to rules of politenefs which
no longer exift. But he was as thorough-

ly

ly impreſſed with the maxim of *place aux dames* as any Frenchman, though without the ſtrain of light and complimentary gallantry which has accompained it in the individuals of that nation. His was a more ſerious ſentiment, connected with the uniform practice of giving up his own eaſe and accommodation, for the ſake of doing a real kindneſs to any female of decent character. It is excellently illuſtrated by an anecdote related in a magazine, by a perſon who chanced to ſail with him in the packet from Holyhead to Dublin, when, the veſſel being much crowded, Mr. *Howard* reſigned his bed to a ſervant-maid, and took up with the cabin floor for himſelf. It is likewiſe diſplayed throughout his works, by the warmth with which

which he always cenfures the practice of putting female prifoners in irons, and ex-pofing them to any harfh and indelicate treatment. He was fond of nothing fo much as the converfation of women of education and cultivated manners, and ftudied to attach them by little elegant prefents, and other marks of attention. Indeed, his foft tones of voice and gen-tlenefs of demeanour might be thought to approach fomewhat to the effeminate, and would furprife thofe who had known him only by the energy of his exertions. In his judgment of female character, it was manifeft that the idea of his loft Harriet was the ftandard of excellence; and, if ever he had married again, a refemblance to her would have been the principal motive of his choice. I recol-

lect

lect to this purpose a singular anecdote, which he related to us on his return from one of his tours. In going from one town in Holland to another in the common passage boat, he was placed near an elderly gentleman, who had in company a young lady of a most engaging manner and appearance, which very strongly reminded him of his Harriet. He was so much struck with her, that, on arriving at the place of destination, he caused his servant to follow them, and get intelligence who they were. It was not without some disappointment that he learned, that the old gentleman was an eminent merchant, and the young lady,—*his wife.*

Mr. *Howard*'s predilection for female society, was in part a consequence of his

his abhorrence of every thing grofs and licentious. His own language and manners were invariably pure and delicate; and the freedoms which pafs uncenfured or even applauded in the promifcuous companies of men, would have affected him with fenfations of difguſt. For a perfon poffeffed of fuch feelings, to have brought himfelf to fubmit to fuch frequent communication with the moſt abandoned of mankind, was perhaps a greater triumph of duty over inclination than any other he obtained in the profecution of his defigns. Yet the nature of his errand to prifons probably infpired awe and refpect in the moſt diffolute; and I think he has recorded, that he never met with a fingle infult from

the

the prifoners in any of the gaols he vifited.

As Mr. *Howard* was fo eminently a *religious* character, it may be expected that fomewhat more fhould be faid of the peculiar tenets he adopted. But, befides that this was a topic which did not enter into our converfations, I confefs, I do not perceive how his general plan of conduct was likely to be influenced by any *peculiarity* of that kind. The principle of *religious duty*, which is nearly the fame in all fyftems, and differs rather in ftrength than in kind in different perfons, is furely fufficient to account for all that he did and underwent in promoting the good of mankind, by modes which Providence feemed to

place

place before him. It has been fuggefted, that he was much under the influence of the doctrine of *predeftination*; and I know not what of *fternnefs* has been attributed to him as its natural confequence. For my own part, I am not able to difcover in what thofe notions of Providence, general and particular, which make part of the profeffion of all religions, differ effentially from the opinions of the predeftinarians; and, from manifold obfervation, I am certain, that the reception of the doctrine of predeftination, as an article of belief, does not neceffarily imply thofe practical confequences which might feem deducible from it. The language, at leaft, of our lower claffes of people is almoft univerfally founded upon it; but when one of them dies

of

of an infectious difeafe, notwithftanding
the byftanders all fpeak of the event as
fated and inevitable, yet each, for himfelf, does not the lefs avoid the infection,
or the lefs recur to medical aid if attacked by it. With refpect to Mr. *Howard*, he never feemed to adopt the idea
that he was moved by an irrefiftible
impulfe to his defigns; for they were the
fubject of much thought and difcuffion:
nor did he confront dangers becaufe he
had a perfuafion that he fhould be preferved from their natural confequences,
but becaufe he was elevated above them.
This fentiment he has himfelf more than
once expreffed in print; and furely none
could be either more rational, or more
adequate to the effects produced. " Being in the way of my duty (fays he),

7   I fear

I fear no evil." I may venture to
affirm, that thofe of the medical profeffion, whofe fearleffnefs is not merely the
refult of habit, muft reafon upon the
fame principle, when they calmly expofe
themfelves to fimilar hazards. *They*, for
the moft part, ufe no precautions againft
contagion: Mr. *Howard did* ufe fome;
though their effects were probably trifling
compared with that of his habitual temperance and cleanlinefs, and his untrou-
bled ferenity of mind. On the whole,
his religious confidence does not appear
to have been of a nature different from
that of other pious men; but to be fo
fteadily and uniformly under its influence, and to be elevated by it to fuch
a fuperiority to all worldly confiderations,
can be the lot of none but thofe who

, have

have formed early habits of referring every thing to the divine will, and of fixing all their views on futurity.

From Mr. *Howard*'s connections with those sects who have ever shewn a particular abhorrence of the frauds and superstitions of popery, it might be supposed, that he would look with a prejudiced eye on the professors and ministers of that persuasion. But such was his veneration for true vital religion, that he was as ready to pay it honour when he met with it in the habit of a *monk*, as under the garb of a *teacher:* and throughout his works, as well as in conversation, he ever dwelt with great complacency on the pure zeal for the good of mankind, and genuine Christian charity, which he frequently discovered

6   among

among the Roman Catholic clergy, both regular and fecular. He was no friend to that hafty diffolution of convents and monafteries which formed part of the multifarious reforms of the late Emperor of Germany. He pitied the aged inmates, male and female, of thefe quiet abodes, who were driven from their beloved retreats into the wide world, with a very flender and often ill-paid pittance for their fupport. " Why might not they (he would fay) be fuffered gradually to die away, and be tranfplanted from one religious houfe to another as their numbers leffened ?" Thofe orders which make it the great duty of their profeffion to attend with the kindeft affiduity upon the fick and imprifoned, and who therefore came continually with-

R   in

in his notice, feemed to conciliate his
good-will to the whole fraternity; and
the virtues of order, decency, fobriety,
and charity, fo much akin to his own,
naturally inclined him to a kind of fel-
lowfhip with them. He rigoroufly, however, abftained from any compliances
with their worfhip which he thought un-
lawful; and gave them his efteem as
men, without the leaft difpofition to
concur with them as theologians.

Such were the great lines of Mr.
Howard's character—lines ftrongly marked, and fufficient to difcriminate him
from any of thofe who have appeared in
a part fomewhat fimilar to his own on
the theatre of the world. The union of
qualities which fo peculiarly fitted him
for the poft he undertook, is not likely,

in our age, again to take place; yet different combinations may be employed to
effect the fame purpofes; and, with refpect to the objects of police and humanity concerning which he occupied himfelf, the information he has collected will
render the repetition of labours like his
unneceffary. To propofe as a model, a
character marked with fuch fingularities,
and, no doubt, with fome foibles, would
be equally vain and injudicious; but his
firm attachment to principle, high fenfe
of honour, pure benevolence, unfhaken
conftancy, and indefatigable perfeve-
rance, may properly be held up to the
view of all perfons occupying important
ftations, or engaged in ufeful enterprifes,
as qualities not lefs to be imitated, than
admired.

I fhall

I fhall conclude with fome account of the *literary honours* which Mr. *Howard* has received from his countrymen. It would, indeed, have been extraordinary, if, while fenates and courts of judicature offered him their tribute of applaufe, poetry and eloquence fhould have fhewn an infenfibility to his merits. Befides the acknowledgments paid him in every publication upon topics fimilar to his own, he became the theme of the elegant mufe of Mr. *Hayley*, who addreffed to him an ode in the year 1780, to which reference has already been made. In the fucceeding year, Mr. *Burke*, adverting, in a fpeech to the freemen of Briftol, to a fact in Mr. *Howard*'s book, ftruck out, with the enthufiafm of genius, into a panegyrical digreffion on his plans and actions,

actions, decorated with his peculiar ftrain of glowing imagery. This fpeech was afterwards printed, and the paffage concerning Mr. *Howard* was copied into various periodical writings, and read with univerfal approbation. His character was even exhibited on the ftage; for a comedy of Mrs. *Inchbald*'s, entitled *Such Things Are*, contained a part evidently modelled upon his peculiar caft of benevolence, which for a time rendered the piece popular.

Dr. *Darwin*'s very beautiful poem of *the Botanic Garden*, printed in 1789, amidft an unexpected variety of fubjects, prefents an eulogium of Mr. *Howard*, fo appropriate and poetical, that I am fure no reader of tafte will require an apology from me for inferting it.

—And

—And now, BENEVOLENCE! thy rays divine
Dart round the globe from Zembla to the Line;
O'er each dark prison plays the cheering light,
Like northern lustres o'er the vault of night.—
From realm to realm, with crofs or crefcent crown'd,
Where'er mankind and mifery are found,
O'er burning fands, deep waves, or wilds of fnow,
Thy HOWARD journeying feeks the houfe of woe.
Down many a winding ftep to dungeons dank,
Where anguifh wails aloud, and fetters clank;
To caves beftrew'd with many a mouldering bone,
And cells, whofe echoes only learn to groan;
Where no kind bars a whifpering friend difclofe,
No funbeam enters, and no zephyr blows,
He treads, inemulous of fame or wealth,
Profufe of toil, and prodigal of health;
With foft affuafive eloquence expands
Power's rigid heart, and opes his clenching hands;
Leads ftern-eye'd juftice to the dark domains,
If not to fever, to relax the chains;
Or guides awaken'd mercy through the gloom,
And fhews the prifon, fifter to the tomb!—
Gives to her babes the felf-devoted wife,
To her fond hufband liberty and life!—
—The fpirits of the good, who bend from high
Wide o'er thefe earthly fcenes their partial eye,
When firft, array'd in VIRTUE's pureft robe,
They faw her HOWARD traverfing the globe;

Saw

Saw round his brows her fun-like glory blaze
In arrowy circles of unwearied rays ;
Miſtook a mortal for an angel-gueſt,
And aſk'd what feraph-foot the earth impreſt.
—Onward he moves!—Diſeaſe and death retire,
And murmuring demons hate him, and admire.

After theſe lines, I cannot be prompt-
ed by vanity in tranſcribing ſome greatly
inferior ones, which, too, have already
been offered to the public. But, as
they were written under the influence
of heartfelt emotions, and refer to the
leading principle of his actions, I hope
they will not be thought miſplaced as
the cloſe of a volume, the purpoſe of
which is to repreſent his character in
ſtrong and faithful colours.

ON THE DEATH OF MR. HOWARD.

Howard, thy task is done ! thy Master calls,
And summons thee from Cherson's distant walls.
" Come, well-approv'd ! my faithful servant ! come;
" No more a wand'rer, seek thy destin'd home.
" Long have I mark'd thee with o'er-ruling eye,
" And sent admiring angels from on high,
" To walk the paths of danger by thy side,
" From death to shield thee, and thro' snares to guide.
" My *minister of good*, I've sped thy way,
" And shot thro' dungeon glooms a leading ray,
" To cheer, by thee, with kind unhoped relief,
" My creatures lost and whelm'd in guilt and grief.
" I've led thee, ardent, on thro' wond'ring climes,
" To combat human woes and human crimes.
" But 'tis enough !—thy *great commission's* o'er ;
" I prove thy faith, thy love, thy zeal, no more.
" Nor droop, that far from country, kindred, friends,
" Thy life, to duty long devoted, ends ;
" What boots it *where* the high reward is giv'n,
" Or *whence* the soul triumphant springs to heav'n?"

F I N I S.

───────────

E R R A T U M.

Page 92, l. 13, *for* where *read* when.